T0329134

Cambridge Elements ≡

Elements in the Archaeology of Europe
edited by
Manuel Fernández-Götz
University of Edinburgh
Bettina Arnold
University of Wisconsin–Milwaukee

MIGRATION MYTHS AND THE END OF THE BRONZE AGE IN THE EASTERN MEDITERRANEAN

A. Bernard Knapp
University of Glasgow

European Association
of Archaeologists

CAMBRIDGE
UNIVERSITY PRESS

CAMBRIDGE
UNIVERSITY PRESS

University Printing House, Cambridge CB2 8BS, United Kingdom

One Liberty Plaza, 20th Floor, New York, NY 10006, USA

477 Williamstown Road, Port Melbourne, VIC 3207, Australia

314–321, 3rd Floor, Plot 3, Splendor Forum, Jasola District Centre,
New Delhi – 110025, India

79 Anson Road, #06–04/06, Singapore 079906

Cambridge University Press is part of the University of Cambridge.

It furthers the University's mission by disseminating knowledge in the pursuit of education, learning, and research at the highest international levels of excellence.

www.cambridge.org
Information on this title: www.cambridge.org/9781108964739
DOI: 10.1017/9781108990363

© A. Bernard Knapp 2021

First published 2021

A catalogue record for this publication is available from the British Library.

ISBN 978-1-108-96473-9 Paperback
ISSN 2632-7058 (online)
ISSN 2632-704X (print)

Migration Myths and the End of the Bronze Age in the Eastern Mediterranean

Elements in the Archaeology of Europe

DOI: 10.1017/9781108990363
First published online: March 2021

A. Bernard Knapp
University of Glasgow
Author for correspondence: A. Bernard Knapp, bernard.knapp@glasgow.ac.uk

Abstract: This Element looks critically at migration scenarios proposed for the end of the Bronze Age in the eastern Mediterranean. After presenting some historical background to the development of migration studies, including types and definitions of migration as well as some of its possible material correlates, I consider how we go about studying human mobility and issues regarding 'ethnicity'. There follows a detailed and critical examination of the history of research related to migration and ethnicity in the southern Levant at the end of the Late Bronze Age (*c*.1200 BC), considering both migrationist and anti-migrationist views. I then present and critique recent studies on climatic and related issues, as well as the current state of evidence from palaeogenetics and strontium isotope analyses. The conclusion attempts to look anew at this enigmatic period of transformation and social change, of mobility and connectivity, alongside the hybridised practices of social actors.

Keywords: archaeology, migration, Bronze Age, eastern Mediterranean

Isbns: 9781108964739 (PB), 9781108990363 (OC)
Issns: 2632-7058 (online), 2632-704X (print)

Contents

Preface

As the chorus of dissent that I expect to arise from this study will surely not fail to point out, I am not a specialist in Mycenaean pottery nor have I ever excavated a Late Bronze or early Iron Age site in the southern Levant (although I spent a few seasons working at the Iron Age sites of Tell esh-Sharia and Tel Gerisa in Israel, and at the multi-period site of Pella in Jordan, during the 1970s and 1980s). Although I have little expertise in Egyptian archaeology and iconography, I was trained in cuneiform – Akkadian, Hittite, Ugaritic – and Hieroglyphic Luwian, as well as other ancient languages peripheral to the present study. However, from the time of writing my MA thesis on the 'sea peoples' while a research student at UC Berkeley (1973), I have maintained a strong interest, read widely, and taught courses in Levantine prehistory, especially that of the southern Levant, and particularly at the end of the Late Bronze Age. Having also been trained from my undergraduate days as an (ancient) historian, I have often observed that some archaeologists, and even more philologists, seem unable to stand back from their specific disciplinary concerns and try to present a broader picture. I hasten to add, however, that many of the archaeologists whose writings and ideas I confront in this study are quite capable historians as well: they simply operate under a paradigm ('the Philistine model') that compels them to see a migration where others see quite different phenomena. Having observed this situation throughout my academic career, I decided it was time to write it up. Those who hope to find the answers to what actually happened at the end of the Bronze Age in the eastern Mediterranean may be disappointed; I will be content, however, if this work succeeds (1) in calling into question the validity of the migrationist paradigm and the 'Philistine model' that emanates from it, and (2) in demonstrating the contradictions that result from adhering to that paradigm.

1 Introduction

We are living in 'an age of migration' (Brettell and Hollifield 2015: 2) and scholars from all areas of history and the social sciences, including archaeology, have become fascinated with what is widely acknowledged as a very complex phenomenon. Those most intimately associated with studying *prehistoric* migrations tend to feel that the main stimulus behind this phenomenon was human agency rather than climatic or environmental change (e.g. Bellwood 2013: 244). Whereas the causes of migration are multiple, complex and often historically specific, the most common explanations proposed in the archaeological literature assume a single, typically generalised cause (e.g. population growth, climate change or other natural disaster, war or invasion, technological developments, socio-economic collapse).

Anthony (1990: 897) commented long ago that archaeologists have 'a paralyzing fascination with the causes of migration, which in most archeological cases is a hopeless quagmire'. People moved or migrated for multiple reasons, but beyond cases of 'forced' migration (e.g. Driessen 2018; Hamilakis 2018), one crucial ('push') factor was the need for new land or access to new marine or terrestrial resources (e.g. for fishing, hunting, farming). Alternatively, where people had the technological wherewithal, the need for such resources might be met by intensifying local production (e.g. opening marginal areas to agriculture), which would have increased land value or encouraged the development of other resources, thus reducing incentives to migrate.

One key problem that arises in studying prehistoric migrations relates to their size; exact figures are in most cases impossible to determine. However, beyond certain known 'mass' migrations (e.g. Palaeolithic or more recent, long-term European colonisations of North America), it is generally acknowledged that – in prehistoric contexts – migration episodes involved relatively small numbers of people (Bellwood 2013: 247). In the case of the southern Levant at the end of the Bronze Age, the subject of this study, there seems to be little awareness of such issues. Stager (1995), for example, imagined a seaborne migration ('Philistines') of some 25,000 people, while Yasur-Landau (2010: 333–4) envisioned a land-based migration involving a minimum of 5,000 to 6,000 people. Such numbers have no basis in material, documentary or historical reality.

Given the general lack of congruence between patterns in language, culture and biology, identifying ancient migrations is a difficult and often controversial task for the archaeologist (Bellwood 2013: 32). Research regarding migrations in the Late Bronze Age (LBA) eastern Mediterranean – whether based on archaeological or documentary evidence, or both – is not only controversial but also tends to be narrow in focus, devoid of theory, replete with terminological inconsistencies, often contradictory, and thus ultimately confusing. Moreover, when Bronze

Age eastern Mediterranean archaeologists engage with the material remains of new 'Philistine' settlements in the early Iron Age southern Levant, or with documentary evidence related to the 'sea peoples', there is a widespread assumption that such settlements were (re-)populated by migrants from the Aegean, Cyprus or Anatolia (or all three). Even accepting that there must have been some level of migration in the southern Levant at that time, only rarely do the associated studies consider just what kind of migration this was, on what scale, and how it may have differed (i.e. what was the 'migration experience'), for example, from other areas in the northern or central Levant, or in Cyprus, Egypt or Anatolia for that matter.

This study attempts to take a fresh, if highly critical, look at notions of migration and mobility at the end of the Bronze Age in the eastern Mediterranean. First, the stage is set by considering some historical background to the development of migration studies, including types and definitions of migration as well as some of its possible material correlates. I also consider some of the interpretative aspects of both migration and mobility, in the attempt to refine how we go about studying migration: while migration obviously involves human movement, mobility is a much more complex and multifaceted process, one that may or may not involve migration. Secondly, I present, on a general level, the history of research related to migration and 'ethnicity' in the southern Levant at the end of the LBA, examining both migrationist and anti-migrationist views. Thirdly, I examine and critique some recent studies on palaeoclimatic and related environmental issues, as well as the current state of evidence from palaeogenetics (ancient DNA–aDNA) and strontium isotope analyses. Following a detailed discussion of mobility and migration in the Late Bronze Age southern Levant, it is argued that most migration scenarios envisioned for the end of the southern Levantine Bronze Age are not only idiosyncratic but also inadequately invested in the wider archaeological, social science, palaeoclimatic and palaeogenetic literature. The conclusion, while ultimately inconclusive, attempts to look anew at this problematic period of transformation and social change, of mobility and connectivity, alongside the hybridised practices of social actors old and new.

2 Migration Studies in Archaeology

As emphasised in several recent works (e.g. Hakenbeck 2008, 2019; van Dommelen 2014: 478–9; Van Oyen 2017), the concept of migration has long engaged the attention of archaeologists, whether positively or negatively. The use of migration as an explanation for cultural transformation has typically been opposed by arguments for indigenous development, diffusion or evolutionary change. Childe (1928), for example, championed diffusionism over migration as an explanation for social change, but he also sought repeatedly to understand how migrations might be identified in the archaeological record (e.g. Childe 1950). Migration and diffusion represent two key aspects of a culture-historical framework; they are seen to provide an explanation for cultural change in prehistory, one that underpins beliefs in the importance of immutable ethnic identities and the boundedness of archaeological cultures.

In general, Anglophone and European archaeological research during the first half of the twentieth century – broadly defined as the culture-historical approach – failed to explain how migration worked or how its archaeological correlates might be identified (Trigger 1968: 39–47). Nonetheless, the culture-historical paradigm has proved to be one of archaeology's most enduring frameworks, one that continues to dominate archaeological discourse in many parts of the world and to shape archaeological notions of migration (Hakenbeck 2008: 12–13). In this paradigm, ethnic groups form the principal actors. Once identified plausibly (or not) in specific material culture assemblages, such groups are tracked in the archaeological record (and associated with each other, or not) and their material patterns are seen as a result of migration or diffusion. Such views of migration typically assume the short-term migration – or 'migration event' – of a specific ethnic or social group (e.g. Philistines, 'sea peoples') that involved major population displacements and long-distance (often maritime) travel, and that had a profound socio-economic and cultural impact on the receiving areas. In terms of method, the culture-historical approach to studying the origin and directions of migrations tends to focus on isolated aspects of the archaeological record thought to be diagnostic in ethnic terms.

Processual archaeologists challenged these methodological and theoretical shortcomings and proposed that cultural development and social change stemmed primarily from internal social dynamics, that is, from systemic factors such as population growth or eco-environmental variability (Clarke 1968: 411–31); this resulted in what was famously termed a 'retreat from migrationism' (Adams et al. 1978). At the same time, island archaeologists sought to develop explicitly comparative, quantitative, biogeographical models of migration to explore cultural patterning, especially in the Pacific and the Caribbean (e.g. MacArthur and Wilson 1967; Rouse 1986). Meanwhile, however, the status of migration as an explanation for demic diffusion, colonisation or cultural change continued to be contested (e.g. Ammerman and Cavalli-Sforza 1984; Renfrew 1987).

By the 1990s, post-processual reactions to such grand scale syntheses began to set in, and archaeologists increasingly engaged with works stemming from the other social sciences to consider the variety, complexity and social contexts of migrations. Archaeological studies of migration thus emphasised some of the following factors involved in migratory movements: transport and economics, demographics and ideology, 'push-pull' dynamics (e.g. Anthony 1990: 899–905; Chapman and Hamerow 1997; Burmeister 2000: 543–4). In turn, Clark (1994) criticised population pressure as an explanation for cultural change, as well as the tendency to equate archaeological assemblages with ethnic groups. Like many others of the time, Clark's scepticism about migration formed part of the processual legacy that rejected migration (and diffusionism) as markers of cultural history and cultural change.

Not long afterward, a growing body of work, initially termed 'archaeogenetics' (Renfrew and Boyle 2000), began to examine migration and the spread of different populations through the interdisciplinary study of genetics, historical linguistics, demographic modelling and archaeological data. More recently, stable isotope analyses of human skeletons have been touted as direct evidence for the movement of individual people (e.g. Bentley 2006; Vander Linden 2007; Nafplioti 2016), or at least of the first generation of migrants (Burmeister 2017: 63–6). Thus, advances in biochemistry – for example, in analysing strontium isotope ratios – have the potential to indicate whether or not individuals were indigenous to the area where their remains were recovered. In turn, geneticists have now begun to compile extensive aDNA (ancient DNA) data sets (e.g. Vander Linden 2016; Feldman et al. 2019; Agranat-Tamir et al. 2020) which, when carefully balanced through interdisciplinary collaboration with archaeologists, have the potential to address key questions about who may have migrated where, and when.

The jury is still out on the issue of just how vital the work of post-processual or social archaeology has been for the study of ancient migrations. There is still some reluctance to consider migration as a research topic in its own right (van Dommelen 2012: 403). Rarely do we find serious engagement with anthropological theory concerning migration, much less any awareness of potentially relevant ideas stemming from economics, sociology, demography, human geography or political science. Anthropologists and geographers, for example, seek to explore the role of social networks and ethnic identity in the movement of people and populations across time and through space, whereas sociologists aim to study the outcome of migratory movements and how immigrants are assimilated, or not, into the receiving society (see various papers in Brettell and Hollifield 2015).

Some recent archaeological approaches have moved away from considering migration simply as a vector for change and instead focus on migration as a complex phenomenon worthy of study in and of itself (Hakenbeck 2008: 21; Leppard 2014; Kristiansen 2016; Burmeister 2017; Leppard et al. 2020). Moreover, the current revival of interest in migration as an explanatory concept is at least partly associated with postmodernist and postcolonial approaches whose aim is to empower the local and indigenous while rebuffing the global and imperial. Many archaeologists, however, still seem motivated simply to demonstrate that large-scale migrations (or invasions) took place without considering adequately the implications of such movements and the range of possible outcomes they typically elicit.

This is certainly the case with the specific episodes that concern us here – the so-called Aegean, 'sea peoples' and/or Philistine migrations at the end of the LBA. Doubts must be raised immediately, however, because archaeologists and especially prehistorians, unlike scholars in other disciplines, confront a unique problem: how can we identify migrants or migrations in the material record in the first place, and how can migration be distinguished from other instances of human mobility? Indeed, this is the crux of the problem for the Bronze Age Mediterranean more generally, as is the issue of identifying the material markers of ethnic identities so readily assumed, argued or passively accepted by many archaeologists.

Migration is a social phenomenon and must be understood as one aspect of human mobility and connectivity, alongside transhumance, exchange, technology transfer, networks, seafaring and 'cultural mobility': it is 'a key constituent element of human life in virtually all periods' (Greenblatt 2010: i) and a 'fundamental part of being human' (Cabana and Clark 2011: 4). It is therefore essential to consider not only the reasons why people were motivated to migrate but also the diversity and complexity of both mobility and migration, and the outcomes for migrants as well as for the communities they left and those that received them (van Dommelen 2014: 480).

Types of Migration

In an edited volume on migration in anthropology, Cabana and Clark (2011: 5–6) observe that people move in two fundamental ways: (1) as individuals or small groups acting independently with a common purpose, and (2) as a larger social group coordinated by a central authority. At a minimum, therefore, migration involves an individual or group of individuals moving from their place of origin to a new – known or unknown – destination on a relatively permanent basis. Such migratory movements may involve crossing a visible material, geophysical or political boundary, or else an invisible, conceptual or cognitive one (e.g. spiritual or mythical movements). Migration thus involves the movement of individuals or social groups between two places that are somehow understood as being different: the movement is therefore not just physical but also social and cultural.

There are many different types of migration that may be related to different social strategies and different kinds of human experience, including attachment to or detachment from a place. These range from brief but repeated movements like those associated with seasonal labour to major diasporas involving the permanent and forced deportation of people (van Dommelen 2012: 404). In cases of 'return migration', people initially move only on a temporary basis (e.g. for work or for reasons of security) but may eventually give up on return movements to their homeland. In cases of 'chain migration', people or even entire communities migrate successively over a long period of time and establish permanent settlements elsewhere; in so doing, they may establish and maintain interregional connections across formal political boundaries that impact on their socio-economic, kinship and community relations (Anthony 1990: 902–4).

Some of the key variables that must be considered in studies of migration include motivation (e.g. push, pull and 'stay' factors), structure and scale (who is involved, and how many people, in what time frame, and what kind of boundaries are being crossed?), distance (geographic, ecological, social), mode (e.g. by land or sea), and the impact on both the immigrants and the receiving community (migratory behaviour) (Cabana and Clark 2011: 6–8). Push factors might include population growth, economic or social breakdown, warfare, the need for new territory, diminished resources or natural disasters. Pull factors may include social or economic advantage, available space, new opportunities or exploration ventures (Bellwood 2013: xv, 2–4, 14).

Considering such variables provides a basic conception of migration linked to a specific research agenda, and thus stands in contrast to approaches that begin with the observed impact and simply infer migration, then work back-wards to identify and categorise immigrants, through their ethnicity for example. Mass movements of people to entirely new and different socio-spatial environments may represent the most dramatic type of migration, but they are rare in comparison with most other known types or with cases where one group of people may co-exist with or be assimilated by another group as a result of migration. 'Migration is an inherently social act or process' that involves crossing both real and perceived boundaries that are socially and culturally, if not politically or linguistically constructed (Cabana and Clark 2011: 9). Because such boundaries may not have clear physical manifestations, any attempt to define them or to determine their presence or absence is fraught with difficulties. Although archaeologists have long sought to discern distinct-ive material boundaries that separate human social groups from one another, even the most carefully contextualised trait lists of material culture seldom provide an adequate basis for establishing a group's social or ethnic identity (Cusick 1998: 137–8).

Migration: Definition and Archaeological Correlates

As already emphasised, migrations are a central fact of social life. While the renewed attention archaeologists focus on migration seems entirely appropriate,

Anthony (1997: 30) argued that it is more important to understand the structure of migratory events than to pursue the actual causes of migration. Migration involves broadly predictable human behaviour 'typically performed by defined subgroups with specific goals, targeted on known destinations and likely to use familiar routes' (Anthony 1990: 895–6). Silberman (1998: 272) echoes this definition, especially with respect to movement, describing migration as 'continuous adaptive behavior between regions with long-standing familiarity, characterized by considerable back-and-forth movement, not a permanent exodus'. Bellwood (2013: 2) defines migration as 'the permanent movement of all or part of a population to inhabit a new territory, separate from that in which it was previously based. Permanent translocation is an essential part of this definition'. Migration, however, is not simply the physical movement from point of origin to destination; it also involves 'a complex swirl of biological, sociocultural, and linguistic activities' and thus may be considered as both a process and an agent of change (Cabana and Clark 2011: 4).

In order to adopt the concept of migration as an explanatory tool, archaeologists need to be able (1) to identify its material cultural traits; (2) to recognise how it works (as patterned behaviour); and (3) to distinguish between the many different types of migratory behaviour that exist (see previous section). Archaeologists typically discuss migration primarily in the context of cultural change, but this focuses on the outcome, not the migration episode itself (Burmeister 2017: 58). In addition, it is necessary to consider what triggers migration, the specific actions involved in such movement (e.g. over land, by sea) and the social processes at work in the destination area (e.g. population density, resistance to incomers, environmental suitability for food production).

What, then, are some *possible* material correlates of migration?

- shared artefact styles
- technological improvements or industrial patterns (metalwork, weaving practices)
- developments in transport (e.g. wheeled vehicles, longboat and sail, ship representations, horse or camel domestication, construction of road networks)
- settlement patterns
- shelter, architecture (houses) and household structure (spatial layout)
- mortuary practices
- symbols, clothing, dress and bodily ornament (e.g. jewellery, headdresses, cosmetics)
- food preparation/cuisine and consumption practices (e.g. faunal remains, fireplaces or hearths, organic residues).

migration – never changes. Stockhammer (2018: 378–9) recently suggested (as already noted) that it should be seen as a transcultural phenomenon:

> In my view, more emphasis should be placed on the process of becoming 'Philistine' through social practices for a particular time at a particular place. It has been demonstrated that 'Philistine' practices could take place within the same building and even side by side with practices that archaeologists would call 'Canaanite' (at least outside the supposed [heartland of] 'Philistia'). The co-existence of Canaanite-type and Philistine-type cooking vessels at the same hearth show that cooking practices of different traditions took place side by side in the supposed 'Philistine' settlements ... . Moreover, 'Philistine' pottery should be understood as a material translation of Aegean style into the local 'Canaanite' spectrum of shapes.

In what follows, the migrationist view (i.e. the Philistine model) is presented in detail, along with some of the problems it raises in attempting to understand the documentary and material records of the thirteenth through eleventh centuries BC in the eastern Mediterranean. To begin with, it should be noted that there is significant disagreement even in identifying the basic nature of the migration process: the Philistine migration and the associated changes in material culture have been seen variously as reflecting such diverse processes as assimilation (Bunimovitz 1990: 219; Dothan 1998: 159), acculturation (Stager 1995: 335; Stone 1995; Gitin 2004: 60, 76), creolisation (Ben-Shlomo et al. 2004: 21), complex diffusion/colonialism (Killebrew 2005: 199–200), cultural fusion (Uziel 2007; Ben-Shlomo 2010: 176), entanglement (Hitchcock and Maeir 2013: 56–9) or transculturation (Stockhammer 2018: 378–80). Little wonder that inconsistency, contradiction and confusion follow.

The Migrationist View

In a series of articles, Middleton (2015, 2018a, 2018b) has critiqued many of the divergent and often conflicting views on the purported Aegean and 'sea peoples' migrations at the end of the LBA. Like him, I take a dim view of most arguments as well as the logic involved in many studies that discuss or defend the notion of such migrations to the southern Levant. In what follows, I trace the recent development of migrationist studies, beginning in the 1980s, and comment on various problems associated with them. I begin with a general overview and continue with a more specific critique of the Philistine migration. In all the sections that follow – both on migrationists and anti-migrationists – my intention is not to be exhaustive but rather to draw on certain studies that may be seen as representative of multiple and diverse points of view.

Overview: Ben-Dor Evian (2018: 219) rightly points out that the migration of Philistines from the Aegean to the southern Levant has become a 'basic paradigm of the 12th century BCE'. But how did this narrative become so predominant? In his attempt to trace the roots of the notion that the biblical Philistines could be equated with the 'sea peoples' of the Egyptian texts (and ultimately with 'Philistine' pottery), and to consider the modern 'obsession' with Philistine origins, Sharon (2001: 556–60) took into account biblical references, classical authors and eighteenth-nineteenth century 'ideologies' concerned with the ways that the 'shadowy civilizations of the East' threatened Eurocentric worldviews. Once European scholars had transcribed the names of Ramesses III's enemies (the 'sea peoples') in the Medinet Habu inscriptions, the *Peleset* (biblical Philistines) – along with the *Sherden*, *Tjekker* and others – assumed an ethnic identity, and the search was on for their historical equivalents, not least in the works of Homer (e.g. the *drdnw* as Dardanians, the *rkw* as Lycians). Having thus established synchronisms among the bible, Egyptian documents and Greek epic poetry, the equivalence of biblical Philistines, Egyptian 'sea peoples' and Homeric Achaeans was secure, and it only remained to determine which Aegean people(s) took part in what was already seen as a 'great migration eastward'. By the early decades of the twentieth century, the stylistic and morphological links between 'Philistine pottery' (Philistine Bichrome) and Mycenaean (Late Helladic) IIIC:1 pottery had become evident, and the question of Philistine origins was regarded as resolved, even if many variations have arisen among subsequent generations of scholars (for a general but still useful account, see Dothan and Dothan 1992: 32–55; see also Sharon 2001: 560–76). In turn, the migrationist narrative took hold, with a seemingly infinite but at the same time increasingly exclusionary variety of scenarios.

The exclusionist nature of the migrationist view is well expressed in the work of Ben-Shlomo (2010: 23–5), in a throwaway section of his book on Philistine iconography, where he states confidently that Philistine material culture may be considered 'a typical case of the connection between "pots and people"' and 'represents cultural elements ... originating from the Aegean and Cyprus, and brought to Philistia by a group of immigrants in the early 12th century BCE'. He mentions counterviews (e.g. Sherratt, Bauer) but states baldly that while such views are not without merit, 'the archaeological evidence continues to support the migration theory, and therefore, other theories will not be taken into account'. Ben-Shlomo thus shows little interest in alternative views and offers no arguments, no archaeological data, no interpretations: he simply asserts an unshakeable belief in the 'conservative or traditional view of the Philistine material culture'.

Most scholars writing from the migrationist perspective share this view-point to some degree, and argue that new, often distinctive material assemblages mark the arrival and settlement of Philistines in the southern Levant (e.g. Dothan and Zukerman 2004; Ben-Shlomo et al. 2008: 226–7; Yasur-Landau 2010; Singer 2012). Some relevant documentary evidence (e.g. Egyptian monumental inscriptions, cuneiform documents, the Hebrew bible) mentions certain events or movements of people in association with tribal names or specified geographic areas. These names (e.g. *Peleset, Šikala, Sherden*) are often taken to be ethnonyms or to represent ethnic identities (see further under *Ethnicity*). Accordingly, some have suggested that while the Philistines settled along the southernmost Levantine coast, the *Šikala* and *Sherden* established themselves farther north, at Dor and in its vicinity (e.g. *Šikala* at Dor, *Sherden* at Akko – Dothan 1986; Stern 2000, 2013; Gilboa 2005: 49–52; Yasur-Landau 2010: 170–1; Sharon and Gilboa 2013: 462–4) (see Figure 1 for all sites mentioned in this study).

In one of her last papers on the subject, Dothan (2000: 156) reiterated her long-standing belief that Philistine material culture was 'rooted in Aegean traditions and adapted to the new environment in Canaan'. She and others have suggested that similarities between Cypriot and Philistine (i.e. Late Helladic IIIC:1b) pottery point to the common origin of Aegean people who settled on Cyprus and in the southern Levant (e.g. Mazar 1985: 105–6; Stager 1995: 336–40; cf. Bunimovitz and Yasur-Landau 1996: 95–6; Bunimovitz 1998).

Based on her own studies of 'Mycenaeanised' pottery in the southern Levant, Killebrew (2005: 219–31) suggested that the Philistine migration may have originated in Cyprus or perhaps in Cilicia or the eastern Aegean, in a context of mobility and interaction (see also Gilboa and Sharon 2017: 291–2). In her view, recent analyses of a wide range of evidence – pottery assemblages, ceramic bathtubs, spool-shaped loomweights, hearths, incised scapulae – find their closest parallels and stylistic ties with 'Aegeanising' features of twelfth-century BC Cyprus, less so with those on Crete and Rhodes or in coastal Cilicia (Killebrew 2018a: 83, 86–7). In another recent paper, Killebrew (2018b: 199–200) is less specific: 'An external material culture, Aegean in style and distinctly different in all aspects from Levantine traditions, also appears during the 12th c. BCE at several sites associated with the Philistines in the southern coastal plain.' Regarding eastern Aegean origins, Mountjoy (2010: 4–5; 2018: 1104–5) has long maintained that the double-stemmed spirals seen on Philistine vessels from Ekron and other southern sites are a regular feature of Mycenaean-type vessels found in that region (the 'interface' of the eastern Aegean and western Anatolia).

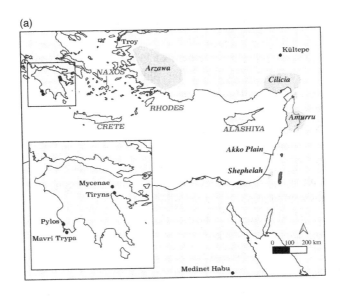

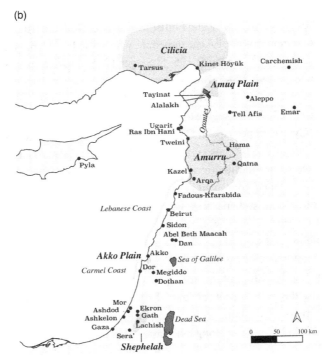

Figure 1a, 1b Maps of Aegean and Levant (drawn by Nathan Meyer).

Others take a broader view, even if they tend to support the notion of an Aegean migration to the southern Levant. A recent study by Bunimovitz and Lederman (2014), for example, is actually concerned with the formation of distinctive Philistine and Israelite identities in the early Iron Age. Nonetheless, it is presented as the aftermath of a migration from the Aegean region: 'Indeed, current excavations in three towns of the Philistine Pentapolis [Ashkelon, Ekron, Gath] endorse the prevailing consensus about Philistine immigration into southern Canaan. . . . The only viable explanation for such a distinct culture change is migration' (Bunimovitz and Lederman 2014: 254). Even so, they acknowledge that archaeologists should attempt to examine the complexity of migration and settlement in a new land, its cultural and political impact on the local population, the meanings of the identities ('self-identification') and post-migration cultural developments as seen in Philistine material culture.

In one of his last papers, Singer (2012: 451–5) discussed 'traditional migrationists' and 'processual indigenists' in the literature on 'sea peoples' and Philistines. The former focus on discontinuity (and invasion, migration, ethnicity) while the latter focus on continuity (and transformation, cultural tradition) – to the latter he might also have added mobility, identity and globalisation. Singer regarded himself as a migrationist and throughout his life argued forcefully for a 'sea peoples' migration (with Aegean origins). Nonetheless, he presented alternative views and considered why they might be attractive, especially those of Sherratt – 'possibly the most eloquent speaker of the indigenist paradigm' (Singer 2012: 451). As Welton et al. (2019: 325) recently pointed out, Singer's (2012: 454–6) traditional views on a 'sea peoples' migration amount to a criticism of interpretations that emphasise continuity and local development; taking into account evidence from the now-extensive excavations at Tell Tayinat in the northern Levant, these authors argue that there is clear evidence for both continuity and change (see further under *Anti-migrationist Views*).

Critique of the Philistine Migration: From the time of her major monograph on the subject, Dothan (1982) was one of the most consistent proponents of the notions (1) that the Philistines migrated from the Aegean to the southern Levant at the end of the Bronze Age, and (2) that their material culture stemmed directly from Aegean traditions adapted to life in this new territory (see also Dothan 2000). Based on materials excavated especially at Tel Miqne/Ekron but also at other Philistine settlements (see map, Figure 1), she argued for 'an abundance of 13th-12th century B.C.E. Aegean connections', and maintained that the transitional Late Bronze–Iron I period involved 'a complex process in which diverse cultures overlapped for certain periods, and that these cultural changes should not be seen as applying simultaneously at all sites' (Dothan 2000: 156). In her view, the first appearance of Mycenaean IIIC:1b pottery at Ekron and Ashdod (dated to the beginning of the twelfth century BC) represented the arrival of the Philistines ('a new cultural element'). Based strictly on three phases of pottery evidence from those sites, she proposed 'three waves of new settlers' (one each for the Monochrome, Philistine Bichrome and Bichrome+burnished red slip) – perhaps the ultimate 'pottery equals people' approach.

True to this tradition, Dothan and Zukerman (2004) argued that the Philistines settled on the southern coastal Levantine plain during the second quarter of twelfth century BC (early in the reign of the Egyptian pharaoh Ramesses III). In this extraordinarily detailed typological analysis of the decoration and technology of locally produced pottery assemblages from the sites of Tel Miqne and Ashdod, their aim was to establish relative chronological links between this pottery and LH IIIC Early-Middle ceramic assemblages from the Aegean, and with the Late Cypriot (LC) IIC and IIIA periods on Cyprus. In that respect, this study represents an attempt to make relative pottery chronology bend to the preconceived notion of the actual timing of settlement. Dothan and Zukerman (2004: 45) maintained that the typology, chronology and regional distribution of LH IIIC:1 pottery refutes the notion that it was produced as a 'substitution' for LBA Aegean imports (i.e. contra Bauer 1998; Sherratt 1998). They associated the abundance of table and kitchen wares in this material assemblage with Aegean/east Mediterranean culinary practices and claimed that – despite the close parallels of the Ekron and Ashdod pottery with that found on Cyprus in LC IIIA contexts – 'The ultimate source of inspiration for the Mycenaean IIIC:1 from Ekron and Ashdod is undoubtedly the Aegean world' (Dothan and Zukerman 2004: 44–5). They had no reservations in relating pottery styles to ethnic groups, and maintained that the differences in Aegean-style regional pottery assemblages on Cyprus, in southern Anatolia and all along the Levantine coast involved a long-term, complex process in which different ethnic groups of ultimate, uncertain (Aegean) origin(s) developed a local ceramic style variant wherever they settled.

Stager (1995), followed closely by Stone (1995) and Barako (2000, 2003), presented one of the more extreme expressions of the mass migration of 'sea peoples' – 'boatload after boatload' of 'war- and transport ships' – to various 'beachheads' on the eastern Mediterranean coast, battalions of some 25,000 displaced marines coming ashore in Philistia to stay. LH IIIC:1 pottery is here termed 'sea peoples' Monochrome', followed in a second stage by 'Philistine Bichrome'. A section on absolute chronology (Stager 1995: 335–6) included no radiocarbon dates but instead relied on synchronisms between Mycenaean pottery and Egyptian astronomical dating, itself subject to ongoing dispute (e.g. Bronk Ramsey et al. 2010; Krauss 2015). In Stager's view, the 'Achaeans' who sacked the coastal cities of LBA Cyprus were the same as the 'sea peoples' who raided Levantine coastal cities from Tarsus (in southern Anatolia) to Ashkelon. All the elements of the intrusive culture identified as Philistine – public architecture, loomweights and weaving industry, hearths, metalworking, figurines, animal husbandry, drinking habits – were traced back to the Aegean.

Although there is to this day no evidence for any kind of harbour installation at the site of Ashkelon (e.g. Raban and Tur-Caspa 2008; Wachsmann 2008: 97), Stager (1995: 342, 345) maintained that 'the Philistines built their seaport ... which must have extended along the coast for almost a kilometre and occupied an area of 50–60 ha [hectares]' and served to export 'the traditional commodities of grain, wine, and oil from Philistia to other parts of the Mediterranean'. Gilboa (2005: 69) has already pointed out the fallacy of any notion of Philistine maritime prominence, which, in her view, has been confused with Phoenician maritime activity. Finkelstein (2007: 519), in a short critique of the notion that the Philistines were ever a maritime power, emphasised that of all the Philistine centres, only Ashkelon is situated on the coast; he concluded: 'there is no clear-cut link between the Iron I settlement system in Philistia and the coast'.

Stager's paper is also the source of the notion that the Egyptians under Ramesses III not only failed to re-establish domination over southern Canaan after the early raids of the 'sea peoples' but indeed could only contain Philistine expansion to the core area of the pentapolis by establishing a *cordon sanitaire* along the traditional frontier of Egypt (Stager 1995: 344; see also Faust 2019: 120). This purported mass migration of 'sea peoples' is said to have occurred during the decade between 1185–1175 BC; it was likened (paraphrasing Braudel) to mere 'crests of Sea Peoples' foam, which the tides of history carry on their strong backs', and resulted from the 'frag-mentation and ruralization' of the Mycenaean and Hittite worlds (Stager 1995: 348). Although widely cited in support of the migrationist view, the combin-ation of fact, fiction and imagination in this study severely limit its value.

Like Stager, Barako (2000, 2003) argued forcefully for a major seaborne migration of Aegean people (as many as 25,000) to the southern Levant, a group defined by common geographic and likely ethnic background. Barako was disinclined to discuss other views, in this case simply dismissing them: 'There is little dispute concerning either the Philistines' place of origin (some-where within the Mycenaean cultural ambit) or where they settled (in southern

Canaan)' (Barako 2003: 165). Stager (1995: 332) was equally if more generally dismissive about 'social archaeologists': 'For this cadre of archaeologists, all archaeology (like politics) is local', and their explanations of internal as opposed to external causes of cultural change is seen to 'justif[y] their ignorance of the broader field of comparative archaeology'.

In a paper devoted primarily to establishing a new, lower chronology for the arrival of the Philistines in the Levant, Finkelstein (2000: 165, 173–4) argued (1) that the processes involved in the 'sea peoples' migration (and those of Philistines from the Aegean or southwestern Anatolia) were longer in time and more complex than previously suggested (at least half a century), and (2) that the migration itself was 'relatively limited' in size. In several respects, this study challenged many of the basic chronological and spatial tenets of the traditional migrationist narrative; Finkelstein suggested, for example, that Egyptian rule in the southern Levant lasted until *c.*1130 BC, that Monochrome ware only began after that time, and that sea and land battles against the 'sea peoples' took place in the Nile Delta. Nonetheless, the author ultimately concurs with the migrationist narrative, inasmuch as the Philistines are 'easily identifiable by several Aegean-derived features in their material culture' (Monochrome pottery, kitchen ware, loomweights, hearths, food practices).

In a follow-up study presented as a direct challenge to the Philistine paradigm, Finkelstein (2007) again called into question the timing of their settlement along the southern coastal plain as well as the fortification of their cities, the notion of a Philistine pentapolis organised in a peer-polity system, and the equation of the 'Iron I Philistines' with those mentioned in the bible. Essentially, he negated the notion of a massive maritime invasion of 'sea peoples', but only downdated (to *c.*1140–1130 BC) the movement of 'a few thousand people' – 'sea peoples', other 'local unstable elements' who partly destroyed or devastated several cities, which were then 'resettled by a mixed population of local Canaanites and Aegean immigrants' (Finkelstein 2007: 519, 521–2). Given the extent of Finkelstein's critique, Bauer (2014: 31) exclaimed: 'Indeed, the durability of the "Philistine paradigm" is so great that even after refuting it point by point, Finkelstein (2007: 521) cannot help but begin the conclusion to his argument: "Was there a Sea Peoples migration to the coast of the Levant? Yes".'

Unlike Finkelstein's more muted views of the Philistine migration, Yasur-Landau has been the most vocal supporter of the notion of an Aegean migration to the southern Levant at the end of the LBA (e.g. Yasur-Landau 2005, 2010, 2012a, 2012b, 2018). At the time of its publication, his major monograph on the subject (2010) provided a much-needed, up-to-date discussion of an Aegean migration in the twelfth century BC. Yasur-Landau brought some theoretical balance to an area of traditionally very conservative scholarship and presented a broad array of archaeological evidence to support his views, including especially material practices – in his view, Aegean in origin or style – associated with the domestic domain or *habitus*: methods of food preparation, cooking, serving and storage (e.g. Aegean-type cooking pots and food/drink-related vessels, rectangular hearths); pottery technology (e.g. non-local kilns, clay sources, firing temperatures); textile production (cylindrical loomweights); vernacular architecture; animal husbandry and subsistence economy (increase in pork or beef consumption; decline in pastoral production); and ceremonial or cultic practices (incised scapulae, Aegean *psi*-type and Ashdoda figurines) (Figures 2, 3).

In his monograph (Yasur-Landau 2010: 313–14), and elsewhere (Sweeney and Yasur-Landau 1999), claims were made of Aegean women depicted in the

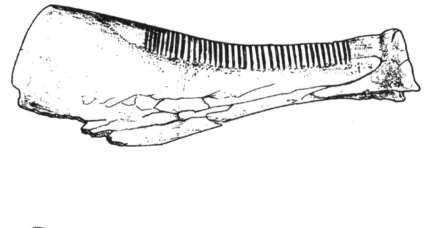

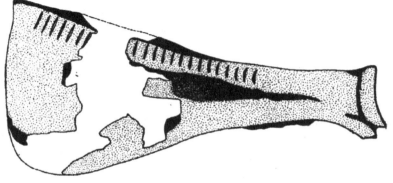

Figure 2 Bovine scapulae from Ekron (Israel) and Kition (Cyprus) (prepared by Nathan Meyer).

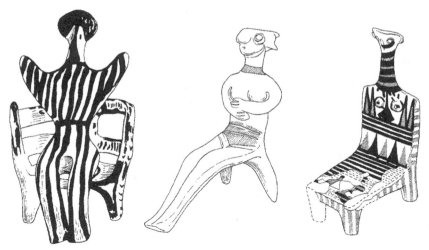

Figure 3 'Ashdoda'-type clay figurines (prepared by Nathan Meyer).

Medinet Habu reliefs, and of Aegean women involved in weaving practices, textile production, cooking and cultic activities. While some of these activities may indeed reflect 'women's work', as Bunimovitz and Yasur-Landau (2002: 214–16) argued long ago, it is also the case that a variety of other factors (e.g. sociopolitical hierarchy, systems of production and exchange, gender and bodily engagements, memory and *habitus*) impact on archaeological attempts to determine past social and material practices. Recent archaeological work on food and cooking practices, for example, tends to de-emphasise gender distinctions and instead focuses on identity, personhood (the individual or the 'dividual'), the social unit (the couple, the family or the community) and *habitus* (e.g. Hastorf 2017). Without specific skeletal, stable isotopic (carbon, nitrogen, strontium) or aDNA data linked directly to women or men in the Philistine material record (cf. Feldman et al. 2019 – see further under *Palaeogenetics (aDNA) and Strontium Isotope Analysis*), assigning gender roles to cooking pots, hearths, loomweights and certain types of figurines remains at best an assumption.

Some of the main categories of material data that bear upon a more nuanced analysis of gender, the body and a binary system of female–male difference are representations of bodies, clothing and bodily ornament or modification, mortuary treatment and burials, sensory evidence (of taste, odours, sounds) and biological evidence of bodies (Robb 2016: ix–x). Research on such categories of evidence is largely absent from the archaeology of Philistia, excepting recent work at Ashkelon on a later (Iron Age IIA) Philistine cemetery with pit burials, built tombs and signs of some cremation (Master and Aja 2017). In that particular case, however, the authors found no evidence of any association between these 'late' Philistine mortuary practices and those of the Bronze Age Aegean or Cyprus; they also felt that Philistine practices differed from burial traditions elsewhere in Judah and the highlands; if anything, there are certain elements that seem to reflect Phoenician practice (Master and Aja 2017: 156–7).

Because Yasur-Landau's (2010) work has become widely cited and is regarded as a sort of primer on Philistine migration and settlement, some further comment is necessary. Despite the evident breadth of scholarship, Yasur-Landau exhibits rather more narrow views on the nature of the Aegean migration (especially to Cyprus), and tends to call upon outmoded theoretical terms such as 'acculturation'. Like many others, he has a tendency to pick and choose his references across all fields, citing those that substantiate his views and ignoring those that challenge or contest them. With reference to Cyprus, for example, he presents his own interpretations of the material but relies heavily on the opinions of scholars whose uncritical acceptance of an Aegean migration to the island has long typified the literature (e.g. Dikaios, Karageorghis, Deger-Jalkotzy); contrasting views are summarily presented but quickly dismissed.

Regarding his main thesis, the Aegean migration to Philistia, Yasur-Landau proposes a massive multigenerational movement of Aegean migrants (farmers and their families) overland *via* Anatolia and throughout the Levant. In his scenario, the resulting 'Aegean aristocratic lineages continued for centuries after the migration' at Tel Miqne and elsewhere (2010: 342). So, the first question that arises is: were they farmers, or aristocrats? Yasur-Landau (2010: 336) estimates that this migration involved a minimum of 5,000–6,000 people (a maximum of 10,000–12,000) and – in a direct challenge to Stager (1995) – suggests that the 'nautical reality' of the twelfth century BC 'makes it highly unlikely that many complete households migrated by boat'. Accordingly, any medium- to large-scale maritime migration to the east would have been virtually impossible. As a possible parallel for the use of land routes through Anatolia, Yasur-Landau (2010: 116) cited the medieval Crusaders. In their movements (not, of course, a migration), the crusaders traversed considerable distances in great numbers, and in so doing not only caused but also suffered many disruptions along the way, not least in their fractious relations with one another. The rulers of towns, districts or even rural communities in this land rarely welcomed people in need of food, shelter and water (Tyerman 2006: 94–100).

The second question that arises is: how easy would it be for farmers (or aristocrats) to migrate, on foot or by primitive cart, from any part of the Aegean world, across all of Anatolia, and south almost to the borders of Egypt? Even if one began this journey from the easternmost point of any conceivable Aegean region, namely the area around Troy in Anatolia, according to Google Maps this trip would have covered some 2,500 km, which would take 513 hours of non-stop walking in a straight line over flat land. In reality, however, such a walk would involve traversing very harsh and often mountainous terrain, and then a coastal plain of extraordinary topographic variety controlled by a medley of different and often hostile polities, all of which makes an overland migration seem like an impossible feat; worse, there is no archaeological evidence to support it.

Although he had his own axe to grind (i.e. a seaborne migration), Barako (2003: 165–6) also noted that overland travel from Asia Minor or Cilicia would have been 'exceedingly difficult' for a large migrating group. In the Levant itself, the coast presents several obstacles: river mouths, promontories, sand dunes, swamps, poor road conditions. Mountjoy (2015: 64, 70–1, figs. 21 & 22) has also written on the difficulties facing anyone attempting to traverse land routes through Asia Minor (see also Jung 2018: 296). Concerning the number of migrants, based on population density estimates (200 people per inhabited hectare) in the southern coastal plain and nearby lowlands (*Shephelah*), Finkelstein (2000: 172) suggested a population of 35,000 in the LBA and 30,000 in Iron I. Because the total built-up area had not changed significantly between the two periods and very few sites were newly established in Iron I, and given the continuity in material culture of the southern Levant at the LBA/Iron I transition, Finkelstein concluded that there was no sign of total population displacement, and that the number of migrants would have been a few thousand at most.

Joining the dissenters, Middleton (2018a: 129) pointed out that a mass migration of thousands of farmers is inherently unlikely: if they had emigrated from Greece to Anatolia and settled down to farm, why would they have moved again, repeatedly it must be assumed if they did so, all the way to the southern Levant? How did these 'migrants' manage to retain their distinctive material culture over generations on the move and, if farmers, why would they have sought to reproduce the material or social practices of an earlier and elite generation in a far-distant homeland from which they had fled? Finally, if climate or other environmental change were a driving (push) factor, why would these farmers make the effort to move from a marginal habitat to an even more extreme, semi-arid landscape? Migrants displaced by natural disasters (disease, famine) have found it difficult if not impossible to undertake the sort of journey involved in a mass migration unless some type of migration network was already in place.

Jung (2018: 296) maintains that it was warlike seafarers who laid waste to sites in the northern Levant, not overland migrants coming from the Aegean via Anatolia to settle in the southern Levant. In his intricately detailed analysis of pottery and metal types supporting Aegean or Italian origins for the 'sea peoples', Jung (2018: 273–5, 293) argues that western migrants sailed in central-Mediterranean-type ships to the northern Levant, especially to Tell Kazel and Tell Arqa. In another recent paper intended as an overview and historical reconstruction of demographic movements at the end of the LBA, Jung (2017) also argued that 'sea peoples' from as far west as Italy – perhaps with an intermediate stay in the Aegean – came by sea to settle in the (central) Levant.

While sympathetic to the suggestion that the appearance of Aegean-style cooking pots and related installations points to the movement of people, not just pottery, Bauer (2014: 33) pointed out that Yasur-Landau did not allow for the role of information exchange (instead of people) as a conduit for the movement of material practices like drinking and feasting rituals. Bauer also criticised Yasur-Landau's notion that the Philistines made and used Aegean-style pottery in its 'original' cultural sense. Citing other recent work, Bauer insisted that LH IIIC1:B pottery (Philistine Monochrome) is entirely a 'Cypro-Levantine phenomenon' with very few production or stylistic links to Late Helladic pottery of the Greek mainland; rather it should be equated with pottery produced on Cyprus or in Cilicia (also Killebrew 2005, 2018a; Ben-Dor Evian 2017: 274; Gilboa and Sharon 2017: 292).

In other, more recent publications, Yasur-Landau (2012a: 38) continued to emphasise 'the reality of the Aegean settlement in Philistia'. In order to explain 'the co-existence of both Aegean and local cultural traditions', he suggested that the southern Levant must have been settled peacefully and by joint agreement between Canaanites and migrants from the Aegean (Yasur-Landau 2012b: 195). It was noted previously that one category of material data useful for a more nuanced analysis of gender and the body is clothing and bodily ornament. In the earlier study, Yasur-Landau (2012a) examined in some detail the 'feathered helmets' found in a variety of media – Egyptian relief sculpture, ivory carving, pottery, seals and scarabs, anthropoid coffin lids – across an area from the Aegean through Cyprus and the Levant to Egypt. He argued that this iconographic element was a distinctive feature of Philistine (and other 'sea peoples') identity and asserted: 'The Aegean occurrences of this headgear support an Aegean origin for the attackers who confronted Egypt during the reign of Ramses III, and, of course, provide further support for the Aegean origin of the Philistines, who settled in the southern Levant at that time' (Yasur-Landau 2012a: 27–8).

Ben-Dor Evian (2015: 67–9) has noted several problems in comparing such a wide range of depictions (of 'feathered helmets') and maintained that they cannot be used to argue for the presence of Aegean warriors in the Levant. She pointed out elsewhere that feathers, at least in Egyptian art, are depicted quite differently from those seen on the 'sea peoples' reliefs of Ramesses III at Medinet Habu (Figure 4); she suggested instead that these elements are reeds, and the people depicted might better be termed 'reed-capped warriors' (Ben-Dor Evian 2016: 159 n.40, 160–3). In the reliefs at Medinet Habu, these reed-capped warriors are seen both among foreign groups within Ramesses III's Egyptian ranks and, in the naval battle scene, as adversaries together with warriors in double-horned helmets. Finally, in a presentation scene, the pharaoh presents prisoners to Amun, including the reed-capped warriors now labelled as *Sikila* (not *Peleset*, i.e. Philistines). As far as the origins of the 'sea peoples' (including the Philistines) and the reed-capped warriors are concerned, elsewhere Ben-Dor Evian (2017: 278–9) concluded that they were displaced populations from (western) Anatolia, Cyprus and the northern Levant (from Cilicia through Syria). I discuss her arguments later but suffice it to say here that her intricate iconographic

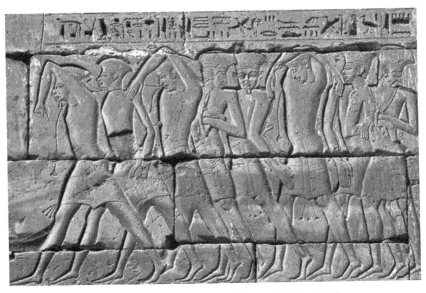

Figure 4 'Reed-capped' warriors at Medinet Habu
(from https://ferrelljenkins.blog/2014/02/10/visualizing-isaiah-9-the-philis
tines-on-the-west/).

analyses of the Medinet Habu reliefs call into question, indirectly but indisputably, Yasur-Landau's interpretations of 'feathered helmets' and the Aegean origin of the Philistines.

Moreover, Verduci (2019: 131–2) points out that the headdress depicted at Medinet Habu should not be regarded as a material marker of Philistine culture, but rather as an aspect of Egyptian culture; similar forms of headwear appear in a wide range of representations, from Italy, the Aegean, Anatolia and Cyprus, as well as the southern Levant. Emanuel (2016: 8–10) also discusses critically the timing and placement of feathered headdresses in the Aegean, Anatolia, Cyprus, the Levant and Egypt. While his overall aim is to show that five anthropoid coffins from Beth Shean in the southern Levant should not be viewed simply as markers of Egyptian or any other 'ethnicity' but as possible examples of transculturalism associated in part with the 'sea peoples', he cites Yasur-Landau (2012a) as an example of the conventional approach that regards this headgear as having originated in and spread from the Aegean world. He points out that the earliest examples of this motif stem from the east Aegean–west Anatolian 'interface' (after Mountjoy 1998), after which it may have spread south to Cyprus and Egypt, and eventually west to the Aegean.

Turning now to other scholars who have presented variations on the main migrationist theme, in an important recent study of metalworking traditions – especially tin bronze production – in the southern Levant throughout the centuries between the Middle Bronze and Iron II periods, Yahalom-Mack (2019) identifies both continuity and change in the metalworkers' toolkit. In particular, she notes (1) that 'a common bronze-working tradition ... spans the Late Bronze Age and the Iron Age I', and (2) that 'at the transition from the Late Bronze Age to the Iron Age, in fact, there is a high degree of continuity in the bronze-working tradition and the accompanying tools', especially pot bellows and tuyères (Yahalom-Mack 2019: 71–2). Similarly, the contents of the Jatt metal hoard indicate 'a continuation of the Late Bronze Age bronze-working *koine*' characteristic of the coastal Levant and Cyprus (Artzy 2006: 97). Although prima facie such findings appear to call into question the presence of incoming migrants, Yahalom-Mack suggests (1) that these metalworking traditions might serve as a proxy to identify sociocultural and ethnic developments, and (2) that the changes seen at the end of the twelfth century BC (Iron I to II transition) reflect a time when 'new people immigrated' and interacted with local populations (Yahalom-Mack 2019: 63–4). Although the issue of migration is entirely secondary in this paper, the author's comments reveal the extent to which the Philistine model is embedded in the archaeological mentality.

Hitchcock and Maeir (2014) have equated the movements of the 'sea peoples' with piratic activities and argue that piracy may have served as a mechanism for limited levels of migration as well as the transmission of foreign cultural traits (but cf. Knapp 2020). Included among these 'disen-franchised' groups of sailors, mercenaries, peasants and others are the *Peleset*, who would have migrated – in limited numbers with minimal mari-time activity – and settled in Canaan. Although they maintain that their argument is not based on 'contemporary theories of Aegean colonization', the material culture of their pirates includes Aegean pottery (for drinking and feasting), iconography and symbolism (Hitchcock and Maeir 2014: 625). On the one hand, these scholars are at times fairly clear that they accept the notion of Philistine migrants, to whatever extent (e.g. Maeir and Hitchcock 2017: 149). On the other hand, they explicitly distance themselves from mass-migration scenarios like those of Stager or Yasur-Landau, and from notions of 'monolithic colonization' by Aegean peoples (Hitchcock and Maeir 2014: 633, 636). Most recently, Maeir et al. (2019: 107) concluded:

> Accordingly, the appearance of the Philistine culture is not the result of a monolithic migration event from Mycenaean Greece, as often presented in the past. Rather, this culture coalesced from various peoples with different geographical, cultural, and sociopolitical backgrounds who settled in Philistia at the end of the Late Bronze/early Iron Age, merging multiple non-local and local social, political, and cultural elements. These groups underwent a process of ethnogenesis, forming an entangled entity that came to be known as the Philistine culture.

Kahn (2011) accepts the notion of a 'sea peoples' migration from the Aegean to the southern Levant, and argues that they were responsible for the destruction of sites in Cyprus, Cilicia and the northern Levant. Like Ben-Dor Evian (2016), he feels that the infamous sea battle described by Ramesses III took place in the Nile Delta but that the land battle took place in the 'Amuq region, around Tell Tayinat (*Palastin*), after which Ramesses III forced the 'sea peoples' to settle in this region, not in the southern Levant (cf. Hoffmeier 2018: 21).

Recent studies by Ben-Dor Evian (2017, 2018) take an informed approach from an Egyptian perspective, although she too supports the notion of a multifaceted migration to the Levant. In her view, the process of early Philistine settlement (i.e. resettlement of defeated 'sea peoples' in the eighth year of Ramesses III) in the region – marked by the presence of Philistine Monochrome pottery – assumes Egyptian involvement, directly or indirectly. Yet this scenario has been difficult to prove in the rich, diverse archaeological record of the southern Levant, specifically with respect to the lack of material evidence for interaction between Egyptian and early Philistine sites (i.e. no Monochrome pottery at Lachish VI, Tel Mor V and Tel Sera' IX; no Egyptian or Egyptianised material assemblages at Ashdod XIII, Ashkelon XVII and Ekron VII). Bunimovitz and Lederman (2014: 255–6) see this conundrum as a material consequence of 'ethnic demarcation': that is, Egyptian and Philistine interrelations would have been strained as the result of strong competition over settlements, and diacritical markers of identity would have a restricted distribution. Thus, the social meaning and significance of LH IIIC:1b pottery and Egyptian(ised) pottery prevented their movement beyond the restricted zones in which they marked identity and cohesion.

For Ben-Dor Evian, however, the main problem is how to reconcile Egyptian historical records with the evident lack of archaeological evidence for interaction between Egyptian and early Philistine material culture in Canaan. Regarding the documentary evidence, she notes that the Medinet Habu inscription, although one of the most detailed documentary sources of the early twelfth century BC, is nonetheless highly ideological in nature with complex formulaic units that render dubious its historical credibility (Ben-Dor Evian 2018: 219; see also Roberts 2009). Archaeologists and ancient historians alike, however, tend to cite various aspects of these inscriptions as historical fact, in particular equating 'sea peoples', the Aegean and Philistia. Ben-Dor Evian (2018: 223–4) suggests that Ramesses III's Year 8 inscription does not refer to lands attacked by the 'sea peoples' (i.e. Hatti, Qode, Carchemish, Arzawa, Alashiya) but instead to polities where the 'sea peoples' served as foreign troops in their armies, thus emphasising the diverse origins of these groups of people. The passage describing the confederation of the *Peleset, Sikila, Shekelesh, Danuna* and *Weshesh* coming with menace towards Egypt may also align with certain texts from Emar and Ugarit (northern Levant), which suggest that land troops inflicted some damage on Levantine polities – Amurru, Mukish-Alalakh, Emar – in the early twelfth century BC. 'Refugees' from the northern Levant then spread to the south, bearing Syrian material traditions: lion-headed cups, geometric motifs on decorated pottery, Philistine ivories.

Ben-Dor Evian accepts that various material elements (Monochrome ware, cylindrical loomweights, rectangular hearths), represent 'new populations' in Philistia but emphasises that they do not appear simultaneously and that the 'main phase of migration' must be later (when Philistine Bichrome appears along with other Cypriot, Aegean, Egyptian and Levantine material traditions). She concludes that the land battles with the 'sea-peoples' took place in the northern parts of Egyptian-controlled territory in the Levant but that the naval clashes probably represent raids on Egyptian sites in the Nile Delta. Thus, the Philistines and by extension other 'sea peoples' were made up of displaced groups coming from as far afield as Anatolia, Cilicia, Cyprus and Syria; they presented a threat to Egypt on its northern frontiers, a threat that was halted in Syria following various site destructions (Tarsus, Tell Kazel, Tell Afis, Ugarit, Ras Ibn Hani). Some of those groups established the kingdom of *Palistin* in the 'Amuq while others eventually reached the southern Levant (Philistia), once Egyptian rule in the Levant declined (post-1150 BC; on the nature of that decline, see Millek 2018). Ben-Dor Evian (2018: 221) thus accepts that Philistines of diverse origins migrated to the southern Levant but that other migrating peoples (e.g. from Amurru in the north) have been overlooked.

In discussing Philistine material culture, Ben-Dor Evian (2017: 271–3) noted that the Monochrome pottery found in sites throughout Cilicia and the Levant has been interpreted in different ways: (1) in Philistia it is argued to indicate an Aegean migration, but (2) in the northern Levant it is regarded as a local cultural process. In this light, and despite the logic of her arguments, it is useful to consider more closely the differences between the two regions and the two processes, i.e. if LH IIIC:1b pottery is viewed as a localised phenomenon in the northern Levant, why should it be taken to represent migration in the south?

Welton et al. (2019: 325) provide at least one possible answer: they suggest that the differences between interpretations regarding the northern and southern Levant at the outset of the Iron Age should be attributed to the diverging scholarly traditions and intellectual histories of the two regions. Furthermore, they argue that these divergent approaches reveal crucial differences in regional material culture trajectories that reflect the remarkable variability typical of these local early Iron Age societies. Their study focuses on the site of Tell Tayinat, abandoned for some 800 years before the Iron I period, when a small settlement became transformed into the royal capital (*Kunulua*) of a kingdom known at different times as *Walastin/Palastin*, *Patina* or *Unqi* (Welton et al. 2019: 292; Osborne et al. 2019: 262).

Tell Tayinat is one of the largest settlements in the Iron Age I northern Levant – at least 10–12 and possibly up to 20 ha in size (Welton et al. 2019: 296). The size of Tayinat, the evidence of domestic vs. industrial activities, the diverse range of material culture, the pottery and small finds, and the presence of luxury raw materials (gold, ivory, carnelian) all indicate a prosperous settlement with extensive interregional connections (Welton et al. 2019: 325). Excavations at Aleppo, some 75 km to the east of Tayinat, uncovered two Hieroglyphic Luwian inscriptions referring to *Palastini*, one of which mentions Taita, its 'hero and king' (Weeden 2013; Hawkins 2020: 44). Another fragmentary Hieroglyphic Luwian inscription from Tell Tayinat itself mentions the land of *Walastini* (Hawkins 2000: 365–6), as does a new fragment from that site which may belong to a colossal statute recently unearthed (Hawkins 2020: 42). Two other inscriptions found near the Orontes river northwest of Hama also mention Taita as the king of the land *Walastini* (Hawkins 2000: 415–19; Osborne et al. 2019: 262). Considered together and with the wealth of material evidence from the site, Welton et al. (2019: 294) argue that Tayinat was the capital of *Walastin/ Palastin*, an Early Iron Age kingdom in the 'Amuq Plain (if not the ancient name of the 'Amuq itself), extending to Aleppo in the east and south into the Orontes river valley (see also Hawkins 2020: 46).

Whether and how *Palastin* may be linked to the *Peleset* of the Medinet Habu inscriptions, and thus to the Philistines, remains an open question (Singer 2012: 466–8). Emanuel (2015: 16), however, has pointed out that if it were not for the toponymic associations and the short-lived presence of Aegean-style pottery in the Iron Age I 'Amuq region, there would be no basis for associating Taita with the Philistines, or with the Aegean in general. Indeed, some of that Aegean-style pottery from Tayinat, which has stylistic affinities with Late Cypriot pottery, shows 'unmistakable signs of independent development' (Janeway 2017: 60, 149). Expanding from their meticulous description of Tell Tayinat, Welton et al. (2019: 294–5) suggest that such evidence as exists for intrusive Aegeanising cultural elements must be offset by equally clear evidence of continuity. They call for more regionally focused discussions of sociocultural continuity and change, emphasising that such impact as the 'sea peoples' may have made cannot be viewed monolithically throughout the eastern Mediterranean.

This brief discussion of finds from Tell Tayinat demonstrates how differently many of the same material phenomena – LH IIIC:1b pottery and its derivatives, loomweights, cooking wares and installations – tend to be interpreted by scholars working in different regions, with different cultural traditions, in the Late Bronze and early Iron Age eastern Mediterranean. At this point, then, it is appropriate to shift focus, and to examine more closely alternative views on the presumed Philistine migration to the southern Levant.

Anti-migrationist Views

Anti-migrationist views have commanded much less attention than their counterparts but are sprinkled throughout the literature over much of the same time period. Drews (1993: 51–3; 2000), for example, argued that the scenes in the reliefs from Medinet Habu do not depict a migration at all; the images of women and children in oxcarts might represent local people fleeing a Pharaonic raid rather than a mass migration of people from distant lands. Kuhrt (1996: 386–7) noted that 'the only sources for the role of the "sea-peoples" in the crisis are the accounts of two Egyptian campaigns' – the rest is the product of modern interpretation and over a century of accumulated scholarship. Likewise, Silberman (1998: 271) suggested that the image of roving invaders originated at least in part from the popularity of invasion fiction, one component of the late nineteenth-century zeitgeist. Both Silberman and Drews felt that indoctrinated ideas about migration should not be divorced from their origins in modern narratives created from the mid-nineteenth century onwards.

Sherratt – a prominent critic of the notion that the Philistines represent a distinctive ethnic group – suggested that Philistine Monochrome pottery (Figure 5) (LH IIIC:1b and derivative wares) was produced and distributed throughout the eastern Mediterranean by a loose confederation of private

Figure 5 'Monochrome' sherds from Garstang's excavations at Ashkelon, 1921. © Ashmolean Museum, University of Oxford.

maritime merchants based in and around Cyprus and possibly Cilicia (e.g. Sherratt 1998: 301–7; 2005: 32–5; 2013: 641–3; 2016; see also Sharon 2001: 592–4). In other words, it was the pottery that moved, not the people traditionally associated with its manufacture (Weeden 2013: 4–5). Moreover, as Sandars (1978: 167–9) once noted: 'It is no good looking for a clue to the "origin of the Philistines" in the pottery. What we find is evidence for an intermingling of peoples from the north among whom an Anatolian element was very strong.'

Sherratt (1998: 294) also argued that it is pointless to focus on the ethnicity or origins of the 'sea peoples', and suggested instead that this enigmatic group should be seen as a structural phenomenon emanating from the international palace-based trade system of the LBA, one that eventually subverted that very system (see also Artzy 1997). In her view, Cyprus became the 'powerhouse' of the ensuing, coastal-based eastern Mediterranean economic and cultural system, with a shared material culture, some of which may have had Mycenaean roots. She regards Philistine Monochrome pottery in Israel as 'a functionally determined selection of the Cypriote White Painted Wheelmade III repertoire' (Sherratt 2003: 45; see also Sherratt 1998: 298). Of course, those who favour the migrationist view pointedly reject this scenario (e.g. Sharon 2001: 592–4; Barako 2003: 164–5; Dothan and Zukerman 2004: 43–5; Singer 2012: 451–5), and maintain that it is not just Philistine pottery that indicates the arrival – whether by land or sea – of a new ethnic group in the southern Levant.

Bauer (2014: 31), however, also contested the migrationists, and put it succinctly: the 'sea peoples' were a 'cosmopolitan bunch' of freelance merchants from Cyprus (if not the Aegean, Anatolia and Levant) whose appearance both affected and resulted from the collapse of international trade at the time. In his view, the types and range of material culture associated with the 'sea peoples' 'reflects a mixture of the many traditions circulating in the internationalism of the Late Bronze Age Mediterranean and represents the emergence of a new social identity out of this international mixing' (Bauer 2014: 34).

As noted, beyond Aegean-style pottery forms and decoration, the sites of the Philistine pentapolis – Ashdod, Ashkelon, Ekron, Gath, Gaza – reveal other, new types of material objects and practices that appear to be quite foreign to local (Canaanite) cultural traditions: figurines and cooking pots (on the last, see Yasur-Landau 2005; Ben-Shlomo et al. 2008), cylinder-shaped loomweights, pebbled hearths (Figure 6) and hearth rooms, incised or 'notched' scapulae, and a striking albeit varying number of pig remains in faunal assemblages (Faust and Lev-Tov 2011: 14–16; Faust 2018; Sapir-Hen 2019; on the other aspects, see also Uziel 2007; Stone 1995).

Regarding lion-headed cups found in various Philistine contexts, Dothan (1982: 231) argued from the outset that they should be viewed as 'the last

Figure 6 Pebbled hearths from late Iron Age I Tell es-Safi/Gath. Courtesy of Prof. Aren M. Maeir, and the Tell es-Safi/Gath Archaeological Project, Bar-Ilan University, Israel.

echo of a long Mycenaean-Minoan tradition of animal-headed rhyta'. Meiberg (2013) revisited this argument in a detailed study of these vessels and found that while they appear to be related to their Aegean counterparts, they are functionally and morphologically closer to lion-headed cups from Middle Bronze Age (MBA) Anatolia (Kültepe) and LBA north Syria (Ugarit, Qatna) (Figure 7; see also Zuckerman 2008).

Based on both material and social practices, Yasur-Landau (2010: 227–81) adopted these ideas and introduced further arguments – based on cooking, serving and storage wares, hearths, textile production, the organisation of domestic space, and more – to support the notion of a more variable and protracted Aegean migration. And, as noted previously, he once floated the possibility of Aegean women accompanying the 'sea peoples' based on the hair style of a woman depicted on the land battle relief at Medinet Habu (Sweeney and Yasur-Landau 1999).

There are multiple concerns about the validity of all such migrationist proposals. For example, given the wide variability within Philistine sites in both the types, shape and placement of hearths, not to mention their possible functions (Maeir and Hitchcock 2011; Gur-Arieh et al. 2012), it seems futile to argue for a single origin in the Aegean (e.g. Yasur-Landau 2010: 234–8). Notched scapulae and seated Ashdoda figurines are most likely Cypriot, not

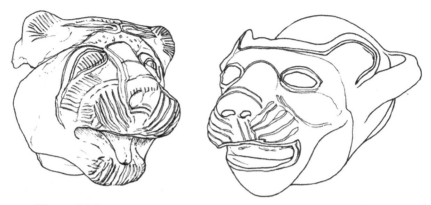

Figure 7 Lion-headed cups from Ugarit (prepared by Nathan Meyer).

Aegean products (Russell 2009; see also Sherratt 1998: 302, n.17) (Figures 2, 3). Regarding loomweights, there are at least fifty-seven sites in the Aegean and eastern Mediterranean dating to the Late Bronze–Iron Age transition with examples; those who have studied these objects most intensively feel that it is impossible to suggest any single region of origin (Rahmstorf 2011: 320–2). And, amongst others, Hesse and Wapnish (1997) as well as Sapir-Hen et al. (2013; see also Sapir-Hen 2019) have argued that the faunal record of early Iron Age is too complex to distinguish ethnic differences based on food preferences (see further under *Ethnicity*).

In a review of a volume on Near Eastern metalwork, Muhly (1980: 160) long ago pointed out that Cyprus had maintained close connections with both the Aegean and the Levant throughout the centuries between 1400 and 1200 BC and that 'one does not need Mycenaean colonists at the end of the Bronze Age to explain the presence of Aegean elements on Cyprus; the same holds true for Ugarit' as well as the southern Levant. Middleton (2018a: 110) also argued that 'Aegeanisation' (in pottery, foodways, textile production) was not a phenomenon restricted to the end of the LBA, but one that goes back for decades if not a century or two on Cyprus and in the eastern Mediterranean. He emphasises, in general, that (1) the material culture traditions of Cyprus and Levant seem much closer than those of the Levant and the Late Palatial and Postpalatial Aegean, and (2) Cyprus should never be taken as synonymous with 'Aegean' (Middleton 2018b: 122, based on Sherratt 1998: 293). As he put it in another, earlier study (Middleton 2015: 46), 'the Sea Peoples' migration and the Mycenaean origin of the Philistines are no more than hypotheses, and are questionable ones at that'. Moreover, and again as Middleton has repeatedly emphasised (most recently

2019: 281), if there was such widespread drought throughout the eastern Mediterranean at this time (as argued, for example, by Langgut et al. 2013; Kaniewski and Van Campo 2017), why would people have chosen to move there en masse?

In another recent paper, Middleton (2018a: 100) suggested that the appearance of novel (Mycenaean or otherwise) features in the early twelfth-century BC Levant might be understood in the context of a 'post-collapse world' in which people – who were still mobile and connected – actively remembered and transformed their heritage. He also cited in this regard the paper by Vanschoonwinkel (1999: 98), who also concluded that 'Mycenaean cultural traits and artifacts' were 'frequently altered or transformed in passage'. Thus, people choose, produce and reproduce their material culture and the ways that they acquire it: such choices are extremely difficult to associate with anyone's ethnic, biological or even geographic origins.

Aegean features are often emphasised in studies on the early Iron Age material culture of the 'Amuq region in northern Syria, and in turn have long been linked to the 'sea peoples' phenomenon (e.g. Janeway 2017). As already noted, however, this phenomenon should not be viewed uniformly throughout the eastern Mediterranean (Welton et al. 2019: 295). Indeed, as Janeway (2017) concludes in his detailed study of Aegean-style pottery at Tell Tayinat, the 'Amuq Valley was resettled towards the end of the twelfth century BC by people from the west who integrated with the indigenous population and together produced a material culture that was at once local, Aegeanising and hybrid. Weeden (2013), moreover, called into question any impact of the 'sea peoples' or other migrations on the polities of north Syria (Carchemish, *Palastin*); as already indicated, he points to both the new Hieroglyphic Luwian inscriptions and archaeological evidence from Tayinat, which show various levels of continuity from the LBA rather than a drastic break. Weeden questions the capacity of archaeology to detect migration on the basis of pottery alone. The pottery and small finds in Iron I levels at Tell Tayinat point to continuity with preceding LBA craft traditions as well as the changes associated with new material traditions: LH IIIC–style pottery (best parallels from Cypriot and northern Levantine coastal sites) and spool-shaped loomweights (Figure 8). The form and fabric of cooking wares, as well as cooking installations, also show continuity with local (LBA) traditions, even if limited numbers of Aegean-style cooking pots also reveal the simultaneous presence of non-local culinary practices.

Maeir and Hitchcock (2017) have outlined the difficulties in trying to pinpoint the ethnic (or geographic) origin of these presumed migrants, or groups of migrants. Once settled, migrants may adapt to various (public) socio-economic or environmental exigencies that define their new world, even if some of them

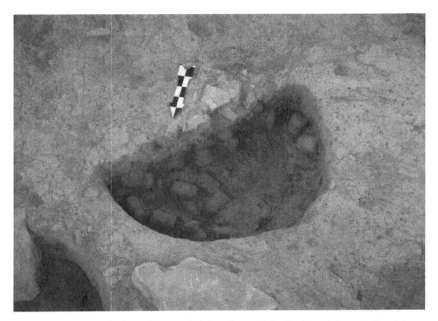

Figure 8 Spool-shaped loomweights from Tell Tayinat (photo D. Lumb).

acquire new meanings. At the same time, they strive to maintain various (private) material and social facets of their old world, daily routines that Bourdieu (1977) defined as *habitus* (Burmeister 2017: 60–1). Such meetings and mixings of people and things might also be viewed in the trajectory of 'third space' (Bhabha 1994: 53–5), one aspect of hybridisation practices. People involved in such practices express their identity or ethnicity at least in part through their material culture. Thinking about migration in terms of hybridisation practices – or entanglement, or transculturation – rather than the movements of presumed ethnic groups enables us to consider alternative perspectives on the dynamics involved in the movements of peoples towards the end of the LBA in the eastern Mediterranean. The subsequent emergence of early Iron Age polities in the region proved to be distinctively different from everything that preceded them in both material and social terms.

    Although anti-migrationists seem to be swimming against an inexorable tide, the concerns they have raised, along with the problems outlined in the present study, should not simply be swept aside. Those who continue to argue for a Philistine migration in the face of such objections need to address these issues directly, not simply follow a satisfying narrative and claim that tradition justifies their stance, or warrants their tendency to ignore counterviews. One of the most problematic issues in migrationist arguments is the notion that a people's ethnicity (Aegeans, Philistines) somehow equates directly to its (their) material culture. On the contrary, it is widely acknowledged amongst archaeologists worldwide that even the most elaborate, detailed and contextualised lists of material culture traits provide no sound basis for establishing an individual's or a group's ethnic identity (Cusick 1998: 137–8). As the following section seeks to demonstrate, although people may choose (and reproduce) the material components of their lives, it is seldom possible to link such choices to anyone's biological or geographic origins, let alone their ethnicity.

Ethnicity

> The concept of ethnicity has been so widely taken up because it gets around the problem of defining what it is that makes a people – that is an ethnos – distinctive. Is the unity it possesses based on language, faith, descent, or culture in some vague sense? Ethnicity covers all as well as covering up all.
>
> (Goody 2001: 8)

In this section, I consider some of the more problematic views of 'ethnicity' that have been used in the attempt to make material as well as documentary evidence 'speak' for migration. I have previously critiqued the concept of ethnicity at some length in at least three separate publications (Knapp 2001; 2008: 35–47; 2014), both as a general concept and as it has been used in studies on the Bronze Age Levant and Cyprus. Accordingly, my discussion here is brief, and focused on ways that this concept has been used, and abused, in the literature on migrations, in particular regarding the end of the LBA in the eastern Mediterranean.

Every archaeologist whose research has focused specifically on issues concerning ethnicity has emphasised an array of problems that must be confronted in attempting to isolate, identify or define specific ethnic groups (e.g. Emberling 1997; Jones 1997; Diaz-Andreu et al. 2005). Because ethnicity is 'something that people do' (Hegmon 1998: 272), identifying its material markers – distinct assemblages of material, recurrent in time and space – poses many difficulties for archaeologists (Diaz-Andreu 1997: 156). Given that variability in material culture results from multiple spatial, functional and other social, political and economic factors beyond ethnicity, most archaeologists harbour deep reservations about linking specific material assemblages to distinct ethnic groups.

Some archaeologists, however, notably those working in a context of literacy like that of the eastern Mediterranean in the LBA, tend to assume that documentary or inscriptional evidence constitutes an key signpost towards ethnicity. Such evidence, however, is often more indicative of elite, top-down perspectives or propaganda that may or may not have some bearing on the identity of the people(s) mentioned. Moreover, we cannot assume that all those who wrote or spoke a single language – e.g. Semitic, Greek or Egyptian – belonged to a single ethnic group (Emberling 1997: 313–15). In any case, multilingualism was probably not uncommon in prehistoric societies – note for example the use of Phoenician, Greek and 'Eteocypriot' on Iron Age Cyprus, or the purported use of Aegean languages/script, Cypro-Minoan, West Semitic, Anatolian and Luwian in the Late Bronze–Iron Age southern Levant (e.g. Gitin et al. 1997; Cross and Stager 2006; Zukerman 2011; Vernet Pons 2012 – all critiqued by Davis 2018). In the case of the presumed Philistine migrants in the southern Levant, the inscriptions number about forty; Davis et al. (2015: 147, 157) concluded that the Philistines must have been multilingual and that it is 'problematic to claim that any particular inscription represents the language, ethnicity, or writing system of the Philistines – or indeed, even to claim that any particular inscription represents the work of a Philistine (rather than a hired foreign) scribe' (see also Maeir et al. 2016: 324–7). The ability to communicate in multiple languages (or scripts) serves as an important mechanism that allows different social groups to maintain certain levels of independence and identity, without one language dominating others (Bellwood 2013: 29).

Notions of ethnicity revolve closely around perception and are only concerned indirectly with material culture. Moreover, there is no one-to-one correspondence between, for example, an ethnic group and a pottery style, as the distribution of pottery (or any other material marker) may indicate political boundaries or the limits of a trading system rather than an indicator of ethnic identity (Hodder 1982: 13–36; Emberling 1997: 311). As already acknowledged, however, some shared social practices reflected in material culture – for example, architecture and household structure, mortuary practices, food preparation and consumption practices, clothing and bodily ornament – may be used in creating social identities and, in some cases, might signify ethnicity or ethnic boundaries. Fashion, clothing and various types of bodily ornament are often associated with the social inscription of the individual; they too have the potential to serve as media for expressing ethnic identity (Comaroff and Comaroff 1992: 74–5). Moreover, in providing origin stories, the memory of migrations is often used to establish or maintain ethnic identities. In encounters with others, migrants often attempt to accentuate various aspects of their identity, but through processes involved in such meetings and mixings – be they termed hybridisation practices, entanglements or transculturation, the identities of migrants and local peoples typically become transformed.

In sum, even if certain material symbols may be expressive of identity and provide indicators of spatial, social or political boundaries, they are typically scarce or difficult to isolate and identify in the material record. Archaeologists who wish to engage with the concept of ethnicity need to explain how ethnic boundaries might have been established, stabilised and maintained through time, and how they might disintegrate or become transformed. Archaeological investigations of migratory movements therefore need to revisit and confront issues related to the formation and maintenance of ethnic groups; such issues are complex enough in recent, historic or ethnographic situations, much more so in prehistoric cases. At best, studies along these lines may suggest the geographic or chronological roots of a particular material assemblage, but they cannot provide direct evidence of the ethnicity or identity of the people who use, interact with or express that particular material form or pattern.

4 Migrations, Climate and Palaeogenetics
Climate and Cultural Change

> The Sea Peoples . . ., that first overwhelmed the Aegean and Eastern Mediterranean empires and kingdoms before hitting Egypt, were probably a flow of migrants looking for *new fertile lands to settle*. Their ranks probably swelled *in each country they crossed, also undermined by climatic stress and food shortages*, during their raids in the Eastern Mediterranean.
>
> (Kaniewski et al. 2019: 2288, emphasis added)

The study quoted here and another recent offering by two of its main authors maintain that the '3.2 kyr cal BP event' (i.e. *c.*1200 BC) represents a period of extreme aridity, a century-scale episode of dry conditions that was the main factor behind the '*huge population migrations* and the decline of ancient eastern Mediterranean civilizations, 3200 years ago' (Kaniewski and Van Campo 2017: 90, emphasis added). In another, earlier paper, the same research group concluded that the LBA crisis coincided with the onset of a 300-year long drought event that 'caused crop failures, dearth and famine, which precipitated or hastened socio-economic crises and forced regional human migrations at the end of the LBA in the Eastern Mediterranean and southwest Asia' (Kaniewski et al. 2013: 9). In the face of such relentless assertions about a direct causal relation between climate crisis and large-scale human migrations, one must ask once again why – if there was such widespread drought throughout the eastern Mediterranean at this time – any group of people would have elected to move from one drought-stricken landscape to another that was 'undermined by climatic stress' (i.e. the eastern Mediterranean), and so presumably was a far cry the kind of 'new fertile lands' in which any migrants might have wished to settle?

In their earlier studies, Kaniewski and his team used palaeoclimatic proxies from sites in the Levant, Greece, Cyprus and Egypt, together with a limited set of radiocarbon dates, in the attempt to explain the 'crisis' at the end of the LBA in the eastern Mediterranean (Kaniewski et al. 2010, 2011). Despite the claims of high-resolution dating, Knapp and Manning (2016: 102–7, figs. 1–3) demonstrated that the dates they provided were sparse, very coarse, and lacked adequate chronological resolution (Figure 9). Such a spuriously precise calibrated radiocarbon chronology as they proposed, within one to two centuries at best, certainly cannot be used to support the supposition of 'huge population migrations'. The most recent paper (Kaniewski et al. 2019) includes ten radiocarbon dates from Cyprus (Pyla *Kokkinokremnos*) and nineteen radiocarbon dates from Syria (Tell Tweini) that more or less correspond with the three centuries in question. Whereas this may be seen as a step in the right direction, in archaeological terms the authors fail to explain what the 'fire events' from Tell Tweini actually are and do not list the contexts of their samples (except that the Pyla samples all come from the same context). In chronological terms, the 3.2 kyr Cal BP event is still framed by 2σ calibrations extending over at least three hundred years (*c.*1320–1025 Cal BC), which hardly help to demonstrate, much less pinpoint, any flow of migrants swelling to the level of a large-scale migration. Finally, all these studies adopt an ahistorical, 'black-box' view to social change: climates got drier and whole societies and economies collapsed, but the actual mechanisms of change are never considered.

Such problems, however, have not deterred others working in the southern Levant from calling upon palaeoclimatic data to argue for large-scale or long-distance migrations. For example, Langgut et al. (2013) generated a detailed pollen diagram from fifty-six palynological samples (sediment cores drilled from the Sea of Galilee) in their attempt to reconstruct prehistoric climate changes; they also employed six AMS radiocarbon-dated samples on short-lived organic material to establish a chronological framework. Having then identified a severe arid phase between *c.*1250–1100 BC, they argued that this prolonged event was 'the most pronounced dry episode during the Bronze and Iron Ages', one that resulted from climatic rather than human-induced change (Langgut et al. 2013: 160). Although the focus of their paper falls upon the impact of climate on collapse, not on migration per se, their view on the latter is clear: 'The long-term climatic changes influenced the stability of the organised kingdoms in the region and led to systemic collapse of the previously well-integrated complex societies in the eastern Mediterranean, depopulation of large areas, urban abandonments and *long-distance migration*' (emphasis added – Langgut et al. 2013: 169; see also 167: table 5).

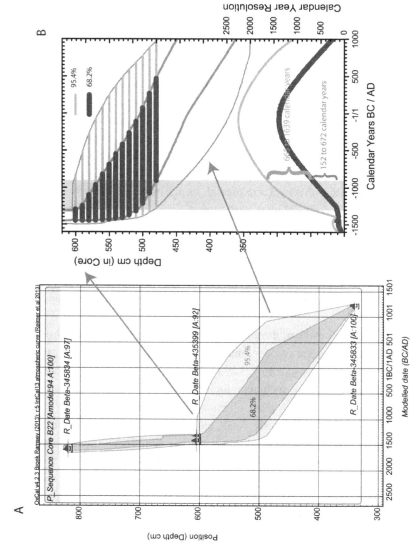

Figure 9 Graph showing the true accuracy and precision of date for Cyprus B22 core (prepared by Sturt W. Manning).

In a subsequent paper by some of the same authors, Finkelstein et al. (2017) focused on (Egyptian) efforts to expand dry farming during the 'dry climate crisis' of the thirteenth and twelfth centuries BC in order to stabilise the situation in the southern Levant. If such efforts were conducted on any significant level, then one must ask – once again – why migrant farmers would bother to move from one marginal habitat (the Aegean) to another that was undergoing a 'dry climate crisis' in an extreme, semi-arid landscape?

Given that climatic change is a complex, multifaceted and multi-scalar issue, Finné et al. (2011: 3154, 3168) suggested some time ago that closer collaboration between archaeologists and climate scientists or dating specialists is essential if arguments are to become more widely acceptable. In reviewing eighteen high quality (but still low resolution) palaeoclimatic proxies spread over the past 6,000 years and using a suite of dating techniques, Finné et al. (2011: 3162, 3167) identified arid conditions in the eastern Mediterranean both before and after *c.*1200 BC. They acknowledged, however, that the proposed climatic date ranges can rarely be resolved to the point they can be related to social or economic crises more closely fixed in time. Despite such concerns, it must be allowed that several proxy databases indicate the possibility of more arid conditions in the Aegean–eastern Mediterranean region at various times between the thirteenth and tenth centuries BC, even if precise dating and thus close association between archaeological data and historical (or migration) 'events' remain an issue.

More recent work in the Aegean specifically attempts to address these concerns. Using new, high-resolution oxygen and carbon isotope data from a stalagmite in the Mavri Trypa Cave (southwestern Peloponnese), Finné et al. (2017) argued that a dry period lasting about twenty years occurred around 1250–1200 BC, followed by a generally wetter if somewhat fluctuating climate that eventually led (*c.*1130–1100 BC) to a distinctively much drier period. However, since the date they suggest for the destruction of the Mycenaean palace at Pylos is around 3150–3130 BP (i.e. *c.*1200–1180 BC), the authors clarified: 'the new paleoclimate evidence from the Greek mainland does not support a clear chronological synchronism between the destruction of the Mycenaean Palace at Pylos and drier conditions, as has been suggested previously' (Finné et al. 2017: 11/18). Weiberg and Finné (2018), citing a wider array of climate data, including from Mavri Trypa Cave, and taking into account a range of archaeological data (from *c.*1800–1075 BC), concluded that whilst climatic volatility characterised the mid-late thirteenth century BC, the twelfth century witnessed increasingly more persistent arid conditions at a time when the Mycenaean palatial system began to disintegrate. Nonetheless, they are clear that 'the long-term perspective offered in this paper shows that there is no unequivocal link between drier climate conditions and societal decline. The outcome of climate stress cannot be determined from the climate conditions alone' (Weiberg and Finné 2018: 596).

In a much broader-based study of hydro-climatic variability throughout the Mediterranean over the past 10,000 years, Finné et al. (2019) observe that the climate 'oscillated' between about 4000–1000 BC (6000–3000+300 BP); at the end of this phase (i.e. *c*.1000+300 BC), they note that the eastern Mediterranean and north Africa became subject to what was, overall, the driest period in the three millennia analysed. In all these studies, Finné and his various colleagues have consistently acknowledged the uncertainties associated with both archaeological and climatological chronologies, which make even very high-resolution correlations problematic.

Such concerns are also evident in another recent paper treating population dynamics and long-term demographic trends in the Levant (Palmisano et al. 2019). While that study is more concerned with agro-pastoral strategies and human-induced impact on the landscape than with climatic change per se, they employed multiple proxies and compared archaeological, pollen and palaeo-climatic data in a multi-scalar approach in order to assess Holocene landscape change. On their broader scale of analysis, they too concluded that (1) 'it is difficult to disentangle the interplay of human and environmental dynamics with a 200-year resolution', and (2) the human response and adaptations to marked climate fluctuations that occurred within shorter time spans would have been immediate, and thus beyond detection at their regional scale of analysis (Palmisano et al. 2019: 722).

Manning et al. (2017: 95) are clear about the problems associated with radiocarbon dating (calibration curve) as well as the palaeoenvironmental issues:

> When radiocarbon dated, a 1200 BCE context inevitably dates from the late 13th century BCE through to the later 12th century BCE – the entire period held to be relevant to the so-called 'crisis years' .... Resolution as regards internal process within this period is therefore a significant challenge. The other fundamental radiocarbon-related problem ... is the lack of truly high resolution palaeoenvironmental evidence in most studies published to date.

As the authors point out, some of these problems can be addressed, for example, by taking multiple radiocarbon dates from the entirety of sediment cores profiles in order to facilitate appropriate (calibrated) age-depth modelling (see also Finné et al. 2017). In the only example they discuss that is of some relevance to the present case, they argue that the overly precise radiocarbon dates published for the destruction of Tell Tweini in the northern Levant – that is, 1194/92–1190 (Kaniewski et al. 2011: 5–6) – fall outside the most likely

68.2 per cent range (1176–1108 BC) and must be regarded as improbable (Manning et al. 2017: 100).

When discussing destructions in the southern Levant, migrationist viewpoints tend to cite case studies like Tell Tweini to justify their own arguments (e.g. Jung 2018: 293). Manning et al. (2017: 108) also point out that the abandonments or destructions at several Late Cypriot (LC) IIC sites, typically linked by many authors with Aegean migrations or 'sea peoples' invasions, were spread over a period of several decades, even up to an entire century, a process that might have involved the climate (more arid conditions) but was probably driven more by politico-economic factors and changing agents and identities in maritime activities.

Finally, it should also be noted that the actual chronology of the Philistine migration is itself the subject of a prolonged debate, concerning not only the specific time – and reasons – that the Egyptians withdrew from southern Levant (e.g. Finkelstein 2000: 161–2; Bunimovitz and Lederman 2014: 253; Millek 2018) but also the varying time sequences (between 50–100 years) and discrepancies in the absolute time frame (over 100 years) during which Philistine material culture appeared at different sites, in different regions (Finkelstein 2016; Asscher and Boaretto 2018; Boaretto et al. 2019).

Concerns over the precision and relevance of palaeoclimatic data and the use of palaeoclimatic proxies are largely absent from the publications of those working in the southern Levant (cf. Langgut et al. 2013). Recent discussions on modelling environmental change are critical of mono-causal explanations; instead they emphasise the complex interplay between human and natural factors in triggering anything from landscape transformation to socio-economic collapse (e.g. Seguin et al. 2019: 151). In discussing an Aegean or Philistine migration to the southern Levant around 1200 BC, or at some point in the century immediately following, the tendency is simply to add climate change to the suite of factors argued for migration. Such views remain problematic, both methodologically and scientifically; assertions about relations between climate change and human migrations require a firmer basis with more convincing data before they can negate alternative arguments, traditional or theoretical.

Palaeogenetics (aDNA) and Strontium Isotope Analyses

To place the study of migration vis-à-vis bioarchaeological data in context, a brief digression may be useful. The reality and longevity of human mobility and migration is demonstrated by the very early peopling of the world by *Homo sapiens sapiens* – be they hunters, foragers or fishers. Indeed, it now seems likely that very early hominins (more precisely, *Homo floresiensis*) may have crossed the Lombok Strait to the Indonesian island of Flores as early as one million years ago, although the earliest skeletal evidence (a mandible and teeth fragments) is now dated ~700 kya (van den Bergh et al. 2016). Within the Mediterranean, maritime dispersals on the order of anywhere from 500 kya–2.6 mya have been argued, contentiously, on the basis of lithics from the Plakias region of southwest Crete (Strasser et al. 2010, 2011; cf. Broodbank 2014; Cherry and Leppard 2018). Other recent work in the Aegean, however, also suggests the *possibility* of purposeful navigation during the Pleistocene. At the site of Stelida on Naxos, for example, excavations in the soil of a chert quarry have revealed over 9,000 artefacts, including hundreds of tools – blades and hand-axes amongst them – in the Mousterian tradition, now dated somewhere between 13–200 kya (Carter et al. 2019). Given varying changes in sea level over this long period, these materials offer potential evidence for the exploitation of these resources by hominins (during lowered sea levels of the Middle Pleistocene) or by *Homo sapiens* of the Early Upper Palaeolithic, the latter quite possibly by sea. Other relevant evidence concerning the likelihood of the very early movement of people to the Aegean islands extends throughout the Palaeolithic (e.g. Runnels 2014; Galanidou 2018), but thus far there is no skeletal evidence from any of these early sites that might lend itself to genetic analysis.

Only human skeletal remains and palaeogenetic analysis can provide direct indicators of ancient biological populations moving through space and time. Both strontium isotope analyses (SIA) and ancient DNA (aDNA) hold out significant promise for identifying prehistoric migrations (Burmeister 2017: 57). Strontium isotope analyses can provide direct, bottom-up evidence for the mobility of individuals, or at least make it possible to identify the first generation of migrating people, specifically to determine whether an individual was native or foreign to their place of archaeological recovery. In turn, genetics and aDNA can inform us (at a statistical level) about populations and thus facilitate the identification of certain groups or individuals that may have been involved in prehistoric migrations (Burmeister 2017: 63–6; see also Hakenbeck 2008: 19).

These relatively new biodistance and bioarchaeological analyses have the capacity to measure specific physical, chemical or molecular features of human remains and thus to estimate precisely how closely population groups or individuals may be linked to specific, geochemically defined regions (van Dommelen 2014: 479). In Bellwood's (2013: 3) view, improving the reliability of migration studies relies on comparing patterns from independent data sets – biology, archaeology, linguistics and palaeoenvironmental sciences – rather than on engaging human biology and genetics alone. However, when used with reliable and extensive (i.e. statistically significant) data sets within an interdisciplinary framework, aDNA analyses have the *potential* to provide new insights into the spread of humans over the globe during the past 50,000 years, and to serve as qualifying arguments for or against specific, presumed episodes of migration.

Some geneticists, however, have made sweeping claims about the ubiquity and impact of migrations in the distant past, none more so than Reich (2018). Many of these palaeogenetic studies have been received by prehistorians with concern (e.g. Mithen 2018; review papers in *Current Anthropology* 59 [2018] 655–62; Hofmann 2019; Furholt 2019). In Booth's (2019: 586) view, the antagonism goes both ways, as archaeological and palaeogenetic interpretations of the same data may not only be different but also are often mischaracterised or misunderstood. Because material culture represents only a proxy measure for demographic mobility and change, Booth (2019: 590) suggests that 'findings from genome-wide palaeogenetic analyses reasonably take precedence over the archaeological record, as the genetic evidence is a direct measure of population change'.

In a more critical vein, however, and like many others (e.g. Furholt 2019; Crellin and Harris 2020), Hakenbeck (2019) argues that several recent studies driven by palaeogenetic research reveal a tendency to revive grand narratives that privilege ethnic groups as agents of historical or prehistoric change. For example, two recent studies involving genomic analyses – and spinoffs from them – purport to show a massive demographic change in the population history of Europe, when an ancestral group of mixed European hunter-gatherers and Near Eastern farmers was overcome and replaced by a group of nomadic pastoralists – ancestral to the Yamnaya culture – from the Eurasian steppe (Allentoft et al. 2015; Haak et al. 2015). This proposed demographic movement has subsequently been reinterpreted as a colonisation of western Europe by roving, predatory, young males (Kristiansen et al. 2017: 339). Furholt (2020: 23–4) points out that, despite the attempt by Kristiansen et al. (2017) to provide a more nuanced and detailed narrative to make sense of these aDNA data, such narratives have repeatedly been deconstructed by both archaeologists and anthropologists over the past 100 years and are now becoming 'repopularized in the context of the new archaeogenetic studies which have had such a profound impact on archaeology' (see also Crellin and Harris 2020: 41, who regard Kristiansen et al.'s [2017] study as 'fundamentally culture-historical in nature'). The notion of static cultures perpetuated in studies such as those of Allentoft et al. (2015) and Haak et al. (2015) not only misrepresents the archaeological record (Vander Linden 2016; Furholt 2018) but also contravenes anthropological understandings of non-state social organisation.

With reference to the same narratives, Hakenbeck (2019: 519–20, fig. 1) points out that the genetic samples chosen by Allentoft et al. (2015) to represent different archaeological cultures map directly onto Childe's 1925 locations of early Bronze Age cultures, and that the samples involved (teeth from 101 buried individuals) are made to stand in for entire archaeological cultures and specific ethnic groups. Whereas some have taken these new studies based on aDNA analyses as a transformational reorientation – the 'third science revolution' – in archaeology (Kristiansen 2014: 14), Hakenbeck (2019: 520) does not mince words in her own reaction to them:

> Rather than being a dawn of new ways of thinking about the past, this is a throw-back to archaeological and linguistic methods of the early twentieth century, by-passing developments that have led to a more critical and nuanced way of thinking about ethnicity, gender and migrations. Instead, we see a return to notions of bounded ethnic groups equivalent to archaeological cultures and of a shared Indo-European social organisation based on common linguistic fragments. Both angles are essentialist and carry a deeply problematic ideological baggage.

She concludes that the research methodology of palaeogenetic analyses lacks theoretical sophistication, notably in considering some of the more complex issues surrounding migration, mobility and ethnicity (similarly, Crellin and Harris 2020). Like many other critics, she cites the methodological problem of taking small numbers of samples of individuals as representative of entire social groups, assuming the samples reflect genetic homogeneity when in fact they may just be obscuring genetic heterogeneity (Hakenbeck 2019: 522).

Booth (2019: 587–8), however, clarifies that the questions being asked are what determines an acceptable sample, and that 'the samples sizes required to address questions of demographic change in the past are smaller than what might be expected intuitively'. A more serious set of problems concerns sample bias, whether spatial, cultural or preservational. Throughout the eastern Mediterranean Bronze Age, for example, the preservation of human skeletal evidence can be patchy or even non-existent and there are still far too few palaeogenetic sample sets published; many earlier studies on the Mediterranean used data from mitochondrial DNA (mtDNA), which is not as robust or informative as whole genome data. This situation justifiably calls into question just how representative of ancient populations such samples might be. Ideally, genetic data should also be supplemented with data from isotopic analyses, as isotopic signatures have demonstrated their value in confirming or negating the likelihood of prehistoric mobility or migration (e.g. Nafplioti 2016). Variable cultural practices like cremation, moreover, might result in a situation where certain ancestries are less visible (if not invisible) archaeologically, or where their remains cannot be subjected to palaeogenetic analyses. Booth (2019: 595), however, concludes on an optimistic if still cautious note on aDNA and palaeogenetics:

> Influential prehistoric population movements obviously have an impact on how archaeologists understand the material record of these periods, but until aDNA can provide more details on how these changes occurred on more local scales, how they may relate to specific material records and archaeological sequences on similar scales, and what this can say about the experiences of communities and individuals who lived in these periods, there is a way to go before palaeogenetics can be said to address an exhaustive range of archaeological questions.

Thus, despite recent methodological advances in archaeogenomic analysis, the crescendo of complaints concerning a range of issues in palaeogenetic research has become nearly deafening. Blakey (2020), for example, ruthlessly attacks the 'biodeterminism' he sees in such studies as indicating the resurgence of pseudoscientific racism amongst the international scientific community. Crellin and Harris (2020: 39) suggest that 'most aDNA analysis rests on an understanding of identity and the human body that is profoundly essentialist, in that it relies on notions of singular and fixed identities that do not reflect the complexity of human lives'. Moreover, with respect to specifically archaeological concerns, even the exponential increase in the number of ancient genomes available cannot allay anxiety over the lack of an informed theoretical framework for discussing aDNA results and the failure to contextualise them better in current archaeological research frameworks.

Eisenmann et al. (2018), for example, argue that recent palaeogenetic studies 'have frequently borrowed archaeological cultural designations to name these genetic groups, while neglecting the historically problematic nature of the concept of cultures in archaeology'. In their paper, Eisenmann et al. (2018: 6) mention the Philistines as an example of naming an archaeological culture after an historically attested and materially discernible group. The spatial equivalence of both the written records and the material evidence drives the assumption that both represent the same group of people; such a connection between past identities and ethnicities, however, needs much closer investigation, not least because most of these identifications, and the corresponding naming of the one (material record) after the other (historical evidence), date back to late nineteenth- and early twentieth-century research practices and the prejudices that accompanied them. Like the work of past generations of culture historians, far too much aDNA research assumes that (1) identity is fixed – for life – at birth, (2) individual identities are strictly exclusionary (e.g. you cannot be both a 'Philistine' and a 'Canaanite') and (3) change can only come about through diffusion or migration (Crellin and Harris 2020: 40). In the face of such critiques, geneticists increasingly are at pains to try and respond to archaeological concerns; some, at least, now seek to align themselves much more closely with archaeologists in order to address 'deep anxieties' about the 'opportunities and challenges of aDNA analysis' (e.g. Sykes et al. 2019: 503).

I turn now to consider the very few aDNA or isotopic studies that may – or may not – have some discernible impact on our understanding of a Philistine or any other migration episode at the end of the LBA in the southern Levant. Only two published studies are directly relevant: one supports the possibility of at least some limited level of migration (and two others are cited as relevant to it), and one argues against migration overall.

Taking the former first, Feldman et al. (2019) extracted and sequenced aDNA from 108 skeletal elements excavated at the Philistine site of Ashkelon, of which ten yielded sufficient amounts of human DNA for analysis. They conducted population genetic analysis on a merged data set, which included published data on 638 ancient individuals and 4,943 individuals from 298 modern-day populations, as well as the genotype data of the 10 skeletal elements from Ashkelon: (1) three from MB IIC-LB II contexts in a Bronze Age necropolis; (2) four from early Iron Age infant burials found beneath late twelfth century BC (Iron Age I) houses; and (3) three recovered from a cemetery next to the city wall of Ashkelon, which was in use during Iron Age II (tenth–ninth centuries BC) (see also Master and Aja 2017). These three groups from Ashkelon derived most of their ancestry from what is termed 'the local Levantine gene pool', as defined in other recent aDNA studies (Feldman et al. 2019: 1, with refs.). The early Iron Age group, however, was distinct in revealing a 'high genetic affinity' to 'European-derived populations', whereas the later Iron Age group revealed no signs of this European affinity.

This study reveals (1) a millennium-long persistence of a local gene pool made up of distinctive Bronze Age Levantine groups from the inland southern Levant (present-day Jordan) and the coastal southern Levant (present-day Israel and Lebanon), (2) a distinctive (European-derived) genetic composition of four infants from early Iron Age Ashkelon, and (3) a local, Levantine gene pool for three individuals from the later Iron Age. Even if we accept the European affinity of the four early Iron Age infants, this genetic signal was weak, and can only have made a limited impact on the population of Ashkelon in the long term. Nonetheless the authors conclude that a 'migration event' occurred at the time of the Late Bronze-early Iron Age transition in Ashkelon, in accord with the arrival of Philistines in the southern coastal Levant (Feldman et al. 2019: 6).

As is the case with many aDNA studies, the number of ancient samples (ten) might be seen as limited, and in this case the 'European-related gene pool' derives from southern Europe generally, not the Aegean specifically. Moreover, the authors do not rule out the possibility that some of this gene flow occurred during the Bronze Age because of 'the limited statistical power of our data stemming from either insufficient coverage or a lack of appropriate contemporaneous proxy populations' (Feldman et al. 2019: 6). They rightly note that additional sampling – e.g. from the wider Levant, Cyprus, the Aegean – is needed in order to characterise better and to identify more precisely any incoming gene flow. Even acknowledging the potential significance of these analyses, however, it still represents quite a leap to go from a genetic analysis of four (out of ten) individual skeletal elements from the site of Ashkelon to a Philistine migration, of any size, from anywhere. The more significant point to carry away from this study is the likely existence of a 'local Levantine gene pool' that spans over a millennium in the Middle-Late Bronze Ages of the southern Levant. A still unpublished study (preprint at https://www.biorxiv.org/content/10.1101/2020.10.23.351882v1) that undertook stable isotope and aDNA analyses of over 150 individuals from Middle-Bronze Age Alalakh in north Syria also reveals a very homogenous, local gene pool, with only five 'non-local' exceptions (Ingman et al. 2020).

Another recent palaeogenomic study also reveals a broadly homogenous 'Canaanite' population during the second millennium BC (Agranat-Tamir et al. 2020). This paper focuses on the Neolithic and Bronze Age southern Levant and involves seventy-three individuals from five Bronze and Iron Age sites, descendant from local Neolithic as well as Chalcolithic Zagros or Bronze Age Caucasus populations. The only two Iron Age individuals in this study – one from Megiddo and the other from Abel Beth Maacah (both inland sites) – revealed ancestry patterns very similar to those of the Middle-Late Bronze Age individuals, leading the authors to suggest that disruptions at the end of the LBA in the southern Levant did not necessarily lead to genetic discontinuity at all sites (Agranat-Tamir et al. 2020: 1153–4).

Haber et al. (2017) also argued that a 'Bronze Age Canaanite-related ancestry' was widespread in the region, at least with respect to people who had inhabited coastal (Sidon) and inland (Jordan) sites. They sequenced genomes from five individuals from Canaanite Sidon, dated to approximately 1700 BC (~3,700 years ago), as well as the genomes of ninety-nine individuals from present-day Lebanon to represent modern Levantine genetic diversity. Once again, there is a limited sample (five) of ancient individuals. The authors maintained that this Canaanite-related ancestry derived from an admixture between local Neolithic populations and distant migrants and concluded that a Canaanite-related population represents the ancestry of most present-day Lebanese. Such a conclusion implies that there has been substantial genetic continuity in the central Levant since at least the transition from the Middle to the Late Bronze Age. Passing over some of their other conclusions, the main point of relevance to the present study is the recurring implication that there has been substantial genetic continuity ('Bronze Age Canaanite-related ancestry') in the central Levant since the onset of the Late Bronze Age.

The second, directly related but more problematic study (Gregoricka and Sheridan 2017) analysed human dental enamel from 543 molars recovered from a tomb at Tel Dothan (Samarian hills) for radiogenic strontium isotope ratios and stable oxygen and carbon isotope values. Extremely limited variability was evident, and the absence of 'non-locals' at the site led the authors to argue that 'population replacement' cannot explain the material or social changes argued by most migrationists. The homogeneity evident among the isotope values points to a community that was not very mobile, which together with regional continuity in material culture over the Late Bronze-early Iron Ages transition led the authors to suggest that such change as is evident would better be ascribed to gradual socio-economic transitions among local populations adapting to hilly environments (Gregoricka and Sheridan 2017: 73–4). To some extent, this supposition may be corroborated by Ullinger et al.'s (2005) examination of thousands of teeth from other Levantine sites, which indicated notable continuity in dental morphological traits of closely related populations within this region. The authors also maintained that continuity is indicated by linguistic evidence for the persistence of distinct Canaanite languages in the region until the mid-first millennium BC.

Strontium isotope ratios and oxygen and carbon isotope values thus indicate that there were no 'non-local immigrants' among these early Iron Age interments at Tel Dothan. Gregoricka and Sheridan (2017: 84) therefore concluded that 'population replacement by invading forces or foreign peoples – comprised of individuals who presumably spent their childhoods in place(s) geographically different from that of the Levant and whose strontium ratios and oxygen and carbon values likely differ from those at Tell [*sic*] Dothan as a result – cannot be supported by this study'. The value of this study, however, is compromised by a couple of points, not least the geographic distance between Tel Dothan and the Philistine heartland, some 75 km as the crow flies. Although both authors are biological anthropologists with wide experience in the Middle East, in this study they failed to draw upon some more relevant (and recent) archaeological studies and, as anti-migrationists they cite, curiously, Finkelstein 1996 and to some extent Hitchcock and Maeir 2013 (they also cite Zuckerman's 2007 article as appearing in the '*Journal of Medical Archaeology*', which actually appeared in the *Journal of Mediterranean Archaeology*). This brings to the fore once again Bellwood's (2013: 3) comment that convincing and reliable studies into any proposed migration episode ideally should involve independent or interdisciplinary specialists – in this case archaeologists – rather than biologists or geneticists alone.

The same problem also seems apparent in a recent study by Matisoo-Smith et al. (2018) which, however, involved eleven scientists as well as six scholars from departments of history and/or archaeology. The data comprise fourteen ancient mitochondrial genome sequences, which, in terms of genetic complexity, can never be as informative as full genomic, aDNA analyses. In any case, these data derive from teeth found in burials at three different sites: one sample from Middle Bronze Age Tell Fadous-Kfarabida (*c.*1800 BC) in Lebanon; three samples from two Phoenician (sixth–first centuries BC) burials found in the centre of modern-day Beirut; and ten samples from Punic Monte Sirai in southwestern Sardinia (sixth–fourth centuries BC). These ancient mitochondrial samples were compared with eighty-seven complete modern mitochondrial genomes from today's Lebanese population and twenty-one ('pre-Phoenician') mitochondrial genomes from Sardinia (note that the twenty-one Sardinian skeletons come from various Neolithic through Nuragic-period tombs, caves and rock shelters). Amongst the many results based solely on the identification of seven mtDNA haplotype groups, which make any resulting interpretation problematic, the authors reasonably argue for continuity between pre-Phoenician and Phoenician populations as reflected in the Monte Sirai Phoenician community. However, they also make several other unconvincing assertions, in particular the likely movement and 'integration of European women in Phoenician communities in Lebanon' (Matisoo-Smith et al. 2018: 15). Although not directly relevant to the issue of a Philistine migration, this study reveals the common tendency to assume that 'both migration and cultural assimilation were common, resulting in surprisingly cosmopolitan communities in the past' (Matisoo-Smith et al. 2018: 15). One could certainly agree, on the basis of all these studies, that mobility was likely a common feature of such 'cosmopolitan communities', but migration is far from evident in the data employed here.

More encouraging is another recent study on Sardinia (Marcus et al. 2020) which, however, focuses exclusively on that island's genetic history and demonstrates how relationships to mainland populations shifted over time. The authors – archaeologists and geneticists working in alignment – generated genome-wide aDNA data for seventy individuals from twenty-one Sardinian archaeological sites that span several thousand years. Whereas all the individuals from the Middle Neolithic (fourth millennium BC) through the Nuragic period (second millennium BC) revealed a strong affinity with western Mediterranean Neolithic populations, individuals from later, first millennium BC Phoenician/Punic sites showed varying signs of admixture with populations mainly from the eastern and northern Mediterranean. Unlike the case with Matisoo-Smith et al. (2018), where the authors argued for continuity between pre-Phoenician and Phoenician populations at Monte Sirai, Marcus et al. (2020: 9) found that eastern Mediterranean ancestry first appeared during the Phoenician-Punic era at Monte Sirai and Villamar: these individuals showed strong genetic relationships to ancient north African and eastern Mediterranean sources. Such results are not unexpected, given that Punic Carthage on the north African coast had roots in the eastern Mediterranean. After the Bronze Age, the southwestern provinces of Campidano and Carbonia indicated more eastern Mediterranean ancestry than the northern provinces of the island (Olbia-Tempio, less so Sassari), where northern Mediterranean immigration was more evident. Such results also align well with known archaeological and historical evidence: the main Phoenician-Punic settlements were situated principally along the south and west coasts, whilst the northeastern part of Sardinia was settled by immigrant Corsican shepherds.

Other, related papers, although like Marcus et al. (2020) not applicable directly to the issue of a Philistine migration, should be noted here, and include the following. In two separate papers that make direct reference to 'sea peoples' migrations at the end of the LBA, Meiri et al. (2017, 2019) examine the aDNA of livestock, in particular pigs. In the earlier study, using mitochondrial DNA of pigs from four sites in Greece and Israel, Meiri et al. (2017: 7) argued that human mobility, whether trade or migration, impacted on the composition of livestock in both Greece and the southern Levant during the Late Bronze and early Iron Ages; they suggested that 'pigs were translocated between the Aegean region, Anatolia and the southern Levant' at that time. This rather cautious conclusion stands in contrast to but is based in part on an even earlier study (Meiri et al. 2013), in which the authors argued that European haplotypes appeared in pig bones from early Iron Age Israel (Iron IIA, *c*. 900 BC), but then suggested – despite the 250–300 year gap – that groups of migrating 'sea peoples' could have brought these pigs to the southern Levant during the Iron I period (*c*.1150–950 BC) (the same argument is echoed in Sapir-Hen et al. 2015: 308–9, 313).

In their more recent paper, Meiri et al. (2019) identify (using aDNA) an Italian pig haplotype from palatial Tiryns in mainland Greece, previously found only in Italy. Their sample consisted of twenty pig (*Sus scrofa domesticus*) and thirty-five cattle (*Bos taurus*) bones and teeth selected from remains found in different areas of Tiryns during the LH IIIB–IIIC periods. Although poor preservation of the DNA hindered any conclusive interpretation of the cattle bones, analysis of the pig bones indicated that European haplotypes began to appear in Anatolia around the end of the Bronze Age, and somewhat later in the southern Levant (also with reference to Meiri et al. 2013). They suggest that this may reflect 'pig translocations connected to various patterns of human mobility and trading activities between the times of the "sea peoples" (early 12th cent. BCE) and the Phoenicians (early first millennium BCE)' (Meiri et al. 2019: 101). They conclude that such 'patterns of mobility' are fully evident in the mitochondrial DNA of pigs, having been translocated by Italian migrants to Mycenaean Greece and other mobile groups ('sea peoples') to the Levant (Meiri et al. 2019: 102). While the movement of pigs with a European 'signature' east and south to Anatolia and the southern Levant also obviously involved people, the mechanism of movement – trade, exchange, livestock replenishment, mobile human groups – cannot be demonstrated with the aDNA data to hand, and certainly cannot be demonstrated on the basis of mtDNA evidence alone. These papers all set out with the a priori assumption that there *was* migration – from Italy to Greece, from Europe to Anatolia and the Levant – and seem determined to prove this phenomenon with the data at hand.

To summarise: aDNA analysis has enabled us to ask (if all too seldom answer) questions that would never even have been raised a decade ago; it has the potential to offer extraordinary insights into past population movements, cultural change, and the associated environmental and social impacts. On their own, however, palaeogenetic studies typically say little if anything about the mechanisms of demographic mobility and change: they may tell us something about genetic change over time, but they cannot explain how and why these changes occur. Issues of identity, which often serve as the implicit focus of aDNA studies, are problematic because identity itself is an inherently messy and contradictory topic (Crellin and Harris 2020: 47). People often hold multiple and entangled identities at the same time: thus, identity is never fixed but always changing, always in process. Moreover, and finally, the size or even the order of magnitude of prehistoric migrations, not to mention a precise timetable, cannot be calculated from genetic data, so identifying 'mass migrations' remains in the realm of the imagination (Booth 2019: 592–3; see also Furholt 2018).

5 Mobility, Migration and the Southern Levant at the End of the Late Bronze Age

Mediterranean prehistory and protohistory encompass a very broad spectrum of 'mobility', which involves diverse if not distinctive kinds of actions and behaviours (see also Middleton 2018b). While Tanasi and Vella (2014: 57, original emphasis), for example, argue at the outset of a paper on islands and mobility in the Bronze Age central Mediterranean that 'the history of the Mediterranean *is* the history of interaction, of the mobility of goods and people and above all connectivity', Woolf (2016: 441) appropriately cautions – in his study of mobility and migration in the early Roman Mediterranean – that '[i]t is not enough to declare ancient populations mobile: we need to consider in what ways people moved and how different kinds of mobility varied within our long historical period'.

Because people move in many different ways, it may be more prudent – at least prima facie – to think in terms of mobility rather than, or in conjunction with, migration. The point is to formulate interpretations of past mobility from the particular to the general, instead of assuming or constructing a definition of migration into which the evidence is then fitted. In the Levant at the Bronze Age–Iron Age transition, arguments for a massive or large-scale migration often have been assembled from local evidence while overlooking the regional situation as well as the relevance of small-scale variations for an in-depth understanding of mobility. Such arguments tend to see migration as a vector for change rather than as a complex phenomenon worthy of study in its own right (Hakenbeck 2008: 20–1).

Clarke (1968) pointed out over half a century ago that archaeological 'cultures' (which in the present case means the material package associated with any migratory group), were not always homogeneous within and sharply bounded without; thus, he argued that they were *polythetic* as opposed to *nomothetic*. Geographic distributions of specific material-culture types are not always coterminous, that is, different kinds of artefacts may have different distributions, depending on their function or how they are associated with a specific social identity. Bellwood (2013: 31, original emphasis) felt that 'material culture combinations are likely to reflect human populations who shared languages and relatively endogamous breeding networks *if* they were complex and internally coherent, geographically widespread, rapid in appearance, and can be inferred to have undergone histories of descent-based (phylogenetic) differentiation'. Material culture alone, in other words, can be misleading when considering evidence for migrations. In the cases of Roman Britain and Indic southeast Asia that Bellwood (2013: 33–5) cited, the archaeological record reveals sharp changes in material culture and associated ideology but no other indications of significant immigration. Only in the case of Anglo-Saxon/Germanic expansion into eastern and central England (sixth–fifth centuries BC) is there evidence for substantial settler migration and/or language replacement. In prehistoric cases it can be difficult if not impossible to determine the extent of migration and/or language replacement when reliant solely on the archaeological record. It may be recalled here that Davis et al. (2015: 147, 157) concluded that the Philistines were likely multilingual and that none of the forty-odd inscriptions attributed to them necessarily represents the language or the writing system of the Philistines, much less their ethnicity.

Middleton (2018b: 120–1) recently proposed that we should move away from migrationist vs non-migrationist arguments – in which mass migration is seen as a 'threshold event' – and instead consider mobility as a means of explaining the movement of various groups of people at the end of the LBA. He defined mobility as a 'temporary or permanent relocation of individuals or small groups ... and their ability to travel'. In his view, mobility is a behaviour that may be facilitated or circumscribed by any individual or group situation within physical or socio-economic systems: some may be able to move more easily than others and some may have more reason (push) or opportunity (pull) to move than others. Mobility is at once a more encompassing and more open concept, and is better suited to consider various forms of movement, from migration of any type to demic diffusion, transhumance, trading and raiding: each type of mobility is determined by and is carried out within specific socio-historical, economic or environmental contexts (Hakenbeck 2008: 19). Many historically attested and contemporary migrations demonstrate that mobility is 'an adaptive strategy in reaction to changing living conditions' (Burmeister 2017: 58).

In his recent compendium on the Bronze Age archaeology of the southern Levant, Greenberg (2019: 274–5) had little to say on the subject: 'the late twelfth-century entanglement of Canaanite and Aegean cultural expression has been widely viewed as evidence for the settlement of LBA "Sea Peoples," later grouped together under the rubric of Philistines'. Pfoh (2018: 62) maintains that those involved in the contemporary study of the transition from the Late Bronze Age to the Iron Age 'still operate under the spell of the biblical account and a barbarian immigration paradigm'. Pfoh was primarily discussing Aramaeans and Israelites in his study, and argued that defining consistent and unambiguous material expressions of ethnic identity in the archaeological record of the southern Levant is riddled with uncertainty; yet even he qualified this by suggesting that 'Aegean/Philistine newcomers' may perhaps represent a 'partial exception' (Pfoh 2018: 64). Once again, the pervasive belief in an Aegean/Philistine migration is evident, even when that belief directly contradicts the arguments involved (in this case, scepticism over identifying self-conscious ethnic identities).

With respect to issues of 'ethnicity', in an early paper, Bunimovitz (1990) laid out in some detail the problems in linking material culture to a specific ethnic group or groups. In his view, 'Philistine material culture' should be regarded as 'a construct of modern research ... a mixture of cultural assemblages that coexisted in Philistia during the 12th–11th centuries B.C.E.'; he argued that such assemblages could not be indicative of any actual ethnic group (Bunimovitz 1990: 201–11). In discussing settlement patterns in the southern coastal plain of Israel, Philistine pottery and cult, and mortuary customs, he pointed out in each case that these elements were either shared widely throughout the southern Levant (pottery, cult) or else likely belonged to specific subcultures, like those of Egyptians or Canaanites (mortuary customs). More recently, he seems to have tended towards accepting the notion of defining ethnic groups in the Iron Age I southern Levant – Philistines, Canaanites, Israelites – although couching the discussion more in terms of 'identity politics' than ethnicity per se (e.g. Bunimovitz and Lederman 2014).

Scholars such as Faust (Faust and Lev-Tov 2011: 18–21; Faust 2018, 2019) maintain that those who lived in rural sites in early Iron Age Philistia cannot be regarded as Philistines because they avoided the use of pork in their diet, and further that pork consumption represents Canaanite behaviour. Thus, it would seem that Canaanites and Philistines were pork eaters, the Israelites were not, and pork consumption (or not) represents an 'ethnic' behaviour. Sapir-Hen (2019) has specifically called this argument into question, noting among other factors that (1) pigs are never the dominant dietary component in the urban centres of Philistia (a high of only 20 per cent at Tel Miqne/Ekron); (2) the dichotomy seen between early Iron Age (Iron I) rural and urban (or highland and lowland) sites in Philistia (Figure 10) probably results from economic rather than ethnic or climatic factors (i.e. pigs were easy to transport and provided a dietary staple); and (3) the purported decline in pig consumption at Iron II sites (down to about 1 per cent in Ashkelon and Tel Miqne/Ekron, much less so at Tell es-Sâfi/Gath), often attributed to the Philistines' 'acculturation' to their new environment, is ambiguous because insufficient comparable data are available. She concluded that pigs cannot serve as an ethnic marker in the LBA–early Iron Age southern Levant (see also Hesse and Wapnish 1997; Sapir-Hen et al. 2015; cf. Faust 2019: 116–117).

To recapitulate a few points: Faust and Lev-Tov (2011) argued that the foreign origin of the Philistines is evident in pottery, cooking techniques (hearths, cooking pots) and an (Aegean) linear script (on the last, cf. Maeir et al. 2016: 324; 2019: 95–6). Yasur-Landau (2010: 234, 267) added to this list new types of cylindrical loomweights and circular hearths that appear in the same sites or areas as Philistine pottery. Other scholars have attempted to link different types of 'sea peoples' helmets, armour, spears, boats or carts depicted on Egyptian reliefs with images depicted on Mycenaean-style pottery and other media (e.g. Roberts 2009; Wachsmann 2013; Yasur-Landau 2013).

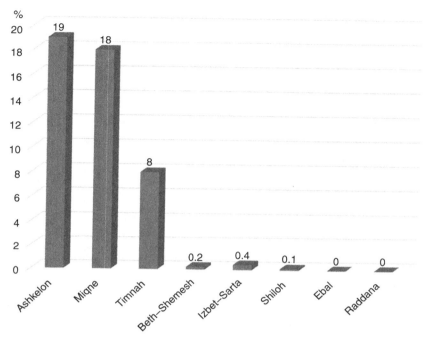

Figure 10 Pig bones in Iron Age 1 Philistia and highlands
(prepared by Nathan Meyer).

If material markers such as four-room houses, collared-rim pithoi and pig avoidance have all been found to be dubious markers of Israelite identity (Gadot 2019: 35), then why should circular hearths, Philistine Monochrome ware and pig usage be seen as valid material markers of Philistine identity or ethnicity? The 'hybrid', Mycenaean-style, Philistine pottery could well be regarded as a localised development in the interconnected world of the early Iron Age eastern Mediterranean (Panitz-Cohen 2014: 550–2), what Greenberg (2019: 274–5) termed the 'entanglement' of Canaanite and Aegean material culture, and thus not necessarily ethnic or even foreign in nature.

Verduci's (2018: 259–62) statistical analyses of metal jewellery from twenty-nine sites in the LBA–early Iron Age southern Levant, Aegean and Cyprus in Iron I-IIA not only points to a pattern of very limited Aegean influence in the southern Levant but also calls for caution in attributing ethnic labels in the attempt to distinguish between strong local and weaker foreign traditions in southern Levantine jewellery (Figure 11). Adornment practices are crucial in conveying information about people's social status, gender and age, even their identity or ethnicity. The material evidence for adornment practices in early Iron

Subtype III.a

Subtype IV.a

Figure 11 Gold pomegranate pendant (Ashdod) and Levantine crescent pendant (Gath) (drawn by Josephine Verduci).

Age Philistine sites indicates clear continuities with local, Levantine traditions, but reveals few attributes of non-local styles or technologies (Maeir et al. 2019: 98–101).

Most archaeologists who have adopted the migrationist point of view still feel compelled to name, assign (ethnic) identities to and uncover the origins of the various 'sea peoples' mentioned or seen in the Medinet Habu inscriptions and reliefs. The Egyptian sources, however, were never intended to provide such neat categorisations (Weeden 2013: 3). Amongst the 'sea peoples' typically cited as belonging to specific ethnic groups or cultures are the *Peleset* (Philistines), *Šikala* and *Sherden* (Bauer 2014: 31). The mention of such groups in the Medinet Habu inscriptions was not an ancient statement on their origins or their ethnicity, but instead served as a rhetorical device, one that addressed the Egyptian (pharaonic) need to conceptualise an external threat. Weeden (2013: 5–6) suggested that this list was likely used to construct an image of Egypt's foreign enemies, and thus points to ways of life – mercantile mobility, small-scale adventurism – on the maritime fringes of the known world.

Some Questions Answered?

Let us return now to some of questions asked at the outset of this study, and try to answer them – at least obliquely – with respect to the case of the southern Levant at the end of the LBA. Foremost among them is how we can identify 'ethnic' migrants or migrations in the material record in the first place. Some of the possible material correlates cited as evidence for a Philistine migration include food preparation techniques, cuisine and consumption practices (e.g. pigs, circular hearths, cooking pots), dress (cylindrical loomweights), bodily ornament (jewellery, headdresses, helmets, armour), shared symbolism or artefact styles (spears, boats or carts compared with images on Mycenaean-style pottery, or Aegean women depicted on Egyptian reliefs), pottery technology (e.g. non-local kilns, clay sources, firing temperatures) and ceremonial practices (incised scapulae, Aegean-type figurines).

Even accepting that objects and installations such as cooking and drinking utensils, foodstuffs, loomweights, hearths and faunal remains, or their associated technologies, represent possible means of identifying an ethnic group, the material in question may or may not be associated with a specific group of people (see also Maeir et al. 2019: 105–7). Such groups continually change their membership, as well as their ideology, materiality and descent; their members often comingled or joined together ('sea peoples'); their names might be passed along to other groups or they might themselves take on new names – actively or passively. Many of the relevant archaeological contexts are ambiguous, and the spatial distribution of specific types of material culture does not enable its unequivocal identification with specific political entities or ethnic groups. Shifts in the distribution of specific material types may be interpreted in more than one way, the problem of equifinality: thus, even if one can track certain material cultural traditions/assemblages, one may not always be dealing with the same ethnic group of people, much less a major migration episode.

Maeir and Hitchcock (2017: 152–5) discuss critically the association of various aspects of Philistine (and other) material culture – hearths, loomweights, pottery decoration, food consumption and especially pigs – with ethnic groups. They argue that non-local features in Philistia cannot be traced to a single origin, and in any case show various degrees of entanglement with local Canaanite material culture (Maeir and Hitchcock 2017: 149; see also Bunimovitz 1990). They maintain that throughout the LBA–early Iron Age transition, much of the southern Levant, far beyond the area of Philistia, was 'in a state of flux and change'; such change, however, was not of an even or uniform character (Maeir and Hitchcock 2017: 151). They conclude that modern, over-simplified – if not essentialising – perceptions of Late Bronze or early Iron Age ethnic groups like Canaanites, Israelites and Philistines are largely based on later written sources (biblical, Egyptian, Assyrian or Babylonian) and may reflect the social or ideological outlook of these later periods.

Another key question raised earlier concerns how migration might be distinguished from other instances of human mobility. During the long period of transition from the Late Bronze to early Iron Age in the Levant, it is possible to see a significant amount of small- to medium-scale mobility (e.g. Aramaeans, Neo-Hittites, Philistines and 'sea peoples', Israelites, Edomites), which may have involved people from the Aegean, Anatolia and Cyprus or from elsewhere within and throughout the Levant. Such human mobility, as well as the material mobility that accompanied it, was a long-established tradition in this region, certainly throughout the LBA (e.g. Cline 1994; Knapp and Cherry 1994: 128–55; Sherratt 2003: 40–51). In Middleton's (2018b: 122) view, people living in those areas of the eastern Mediterranean where imported Mycenaean pottery is attested had been 'consumers' of Mycenaean culture long before 1200 BC, and the appearance of locally made Mycenaean wares in the southern Levant should be seen in such a context of long-term mobility and connectivity. Beyond this long history of mobility, sociopolitical developments in the early Iron Age – the loosening of state control after the end of the LBA, increasingly flexible economic structures – may have incited more movement(s) than in previous periods and offered more incentives (both push and pull factors) for movement.

Such documentary and iconographic evidence as exists (programmatic royal inscriptions, relief carvings, etc.) never refers directly to distinct and unidirec-tional migrations, but instead mentions diverse groups and individuals – traders, raiders, craft specialists, 'high status' people, refugees – moving, settling, trading, intermarrying, and working in multiple places, for manifold reasons, whether temporarily or permanently (e.g. Killebrew 2005: 202–5; Adams and Cohen 2013; Knapp and Manning 2016: 118–23; Middleton 2018b: 131). Although relevant archaeological evidence appears to be widespread (if often misleading), the material contexts of mobility or migration tend to be ambigu-ous and the spatial distribution of material – typically ceramic – traits often used to identify different cultures and even to reconstruct ethnic groups remains equivocal and subject to different interpretations. The recent paper by Raneri et al. (2019) on 'sea people', for example, not only proposes – on the basis of problematic provenance analyses (petrographic and chemical data inadequately aligned) – to have identified an 'Aegeanizing ceramic production' at Tell Afis along the north Syrian coast but also considers such production to be linked to 'sea people culture'. This paper is problematic not only with respect to science-based archaeology but also in the way it represents ancient 'culture'.

Leppard et al. (2020: 215) have emphasised that human mobility is complex and multidimensional: 'all migration is mobility but not all mobility is migration'. In their view, migration may be comparatively easy to trace but mobility, which occurs across multidimensional scales, is harder to grasp. More importantly for the present discussion is their finding – using a meta-analysis of strontium isotope ($87Sr/86Sr$) data derived from funerary populations across the Neolithic to Late Roman Mediterranean (899 samples) – that less than 10 per cent of these individuals were 'non-local' in origin (using the statistically most robust data set [702 samples], the mean non-local rate dropped to only 5.84 per cent). In the authors' view, even this likely represents an overestimate. The mortuary record they analysed covers a broad social range, from the royal burials in Grave Circle A at Bronze Age Mycenae to low-status cemeteries on the outskirts of imperial Rome. The overall temporal trend shows comparatively higher levels of mobility in the Neolithic (*c.*7000–3500 BC) that decrease over time. The authors also stress that in some cases where high levels of in-migration might be expected on the basis of notable changes in material culture (e.g. at the Middle to Late Minoan transition on Crete, or the Late Bronze to Iron Age transition in the eastern Mediterranean), there is little bioarchaeological evidence of non-locals. While these results stem from pioneering work and may be expected to change with the inclusion of more data, they clearly present a challenge to the notion of a highly connected Mediterranean with people perpetually in motion.

Turning to consider reasons that might have motivated people to migrate and what kinds of mobility were involved, as already noted Maeir and Hitchcock (2017: 151) suggested that although various components of Philistine culture (and its population) may be of non-local origin, such foreign traits were mixed – revealing features known from Cyprus, Anatolia, the Aegean, southeastern Europe and beyond – and thus indicate multiple origins of the people who ultimately became integrated with local Canaanite populations. They accept that there was an 'influx of foreign immigrants' but maintain that 'the origins of the Philistine culture cannot be explained as a monolithic migration of peoples of Mycenaean origin' (Maeir and Hitchcock 2017: 149, 151 n.1). The corollary of multiple origins, of course, is that there were also very likely multiple mechanisms (e.g. push-pull factors, economics of transport, demographic factors) and different vectors of mobility (e.g. mercantile, social and maritime networks, technology transfer, forced mobility) that brought new people to the southern Levant at the outset of the early Iron Age.

Most archaeologists – migrationists as well as non-migrationists – would probably agree that the heightened human mobility evident in the early Iron Age resulted at least in part from the disruptions to the strongly centralised economies of the LBA Aegean and eastern Mediterranean, the abandonment and in some cases destruction of many coastal settlements, and the attendant collapse of multiple kingdoms and city states (e.g. the Hittite state, the Cypriot polity, the Ugaritic kingdom and other Levantine city states). As far as sea transport is concerned, LBA developments in maritime technology may well have facilitated human mobiliy (Emanuel 2016: 271–2).

Beyond politico-economic or social breakdown, other push factors might include population growth and the need for new land or access to new marine or other resources (although there is no definitive material or documentary evidence for these), diminished resources or natural disasters (the evidence is controversial), and of course climate change (many claims made but inadequate data to verify them). In other cases, pull factors might include new social or economic opportunities or more space available to establish a new community, but it is difficult to see how the semi-arid landscape of the (in this case, restricted) southern Levantine coastal zone would have held out much attraction, except possibly in cases of forced migration. As Killebrew (2018b: 199) observed: 'there is no evidence of long-distance forced migration in the archaeological record of the southern Levant, rather local dislocations and resettlements of displaced peoples'. In her view, the 'newcomers' to Philistia (Ekron in particular) were not refugees or immigrants but a well-organised group of colonists who would have integrated the local (Canaanite) population into their newly established town. Ben-Dor Evian (2018: 221) also proposed that 'Syrian refugees' fleeing from ('sea peoples') attacks 'spread across the southern Levant as well, bringing with them Syrian traditions' (lion-headed cups, various geometric motifs on decorated pottery, temple plans, Philistine ivories): the impetus here, of course, is on forced migration as a reaction to (presumed) military aggression, but if accepted as a valid scenario could be seen as a new opportunity.

This brings us to the final question: what were the outcomes for people on the move (migrants or not) towards the end of the LBA and beginning of the Iron Age, as well as for the communities that received them or those they left behind? Although Gilboa and Sharon (2017: 285) suggested that the investigation of phenomena associated with migrating 'sea peoples' has shifted from questions of geographic origin and ethnicity to issues of identity formation and the 'social dialectics' between immigrants and local people, the reality remains rather mixed.

From a somewhat muted migrationist perspective, Bunimovitz and Lederman (2014: 256–61) examined the cultural and political impact of Philistine migrants on the local Canaanite population as seen in material culture and settlement patterning developments. They interpret the precipitous drop in settlement sites on the southern coastal plain and neighbouring lowlands (*Shephelah*) during Iron Age I (Finkelstein 1996, 2000) as reflecting an intentional displacement of the local rural (Canaanite) population into the main Philistine centres. By contrast, settlements located farther distant from these centres seem to have avoided what they term an 'hostile takeover' (see also Bunimovitz 1998: 107–8). However, they also view the effects of Philistine–Canaanite interaction on certain aspects of the material culture – cooking pots, perforated cylinder-shaped loomweights, iconography – as indicative of hybridisation practices, suggesting that some innovations related to the domestic sphere (loomweights, cooking pots) may have resulted from intercultural marriage whereas others led to changes in local behavioral patterns (Bunimovitz and Lederman 2014: 257).

Beyond the Philistine core area, however, Canaanite cultural traditions persisted, in architecture, pottery and bronze production and more, while the locally produced Bichrome Philistine pottery is absent (Bunimovitz and Lederman 2014: 259, fig. 14.6). In sum, they maintain that those Canaanites who lived in the southern coastal plain and neighbouring foothills forcibly came under Philistine rule while those living in the periphery resisted Philistine pressure and expansion. They summarise eloquently their views on the social processes at work in the destination area: 'Like a stone thrown into a pond of still water, the Philistines aroused a series of concentric waves of cultural dialogues in which they and the local Canaanite population were involved. The end result of these dialogues . . . was hybridization in heartland Philistia, resistance on its border zone, and ethnogenesis in the highlands' (Bunimovitz and Lederman 2014: 261).

Of course, thinking about migration in terms of hybridisation practices behoves us to consider alternative perspectives concerning the movements of people during the LBA–early Iron Age transition in the eastern Mediterranean. Throughout the Levant, the emergence of early Iron Age polities looks distinctively different from everything that preceded them, in material, social and politico-economic terms. The contrast between the political economies of most Levantine LBA and early Iron Age polities is widely viewed as a new development in Iron Age state formation, despite similarities and differences in their structuring principles. For example, although Phoenician polities are typically regarded as the direct successors of the Canaanite city states (e.g. Aubet 2001), both archaeological as well as documentary records reveal very different, more complex situations (Gilboa and Sharon 2017; Monroe 2018; Sader 2019: 23–49).

The structural diversity of all these early Iron Age polities means that most scholars who study them have developed local typologies to account for their diversity (Routledge 2017: 59–60). Joffe (2002), for example, viewed the (somewhat later) Iron Age southern Levantine kingdoms as 'ethnic states' whose integration followed rather than preceded state formation. In the northern Levant, rulers seldom exercised their full authority over the territories they claimed (Osborne 2013). In Routledge's (2017: 66) view, state formation in the Iron Age Levant was a work of 'bricolage', not the unfolding of some ethnic movements or other, predetermined sociohistorical processes. Thus, all along the Levantine seaboard, diverse communities were transformed as resource acquisition strategies broke down, regional states declined and populations shifted and moved. New relations of power had to be established and legitimised within specific spatial and historical contexts.

Turning specifically to the southern Levant, anti-migrationists predictably have different views on just what took place at the end of the LBA. Emphasising the futility of focusing on the ethnicity or origins of the 'sea peoples', Sherratt (1998: 294, 301–7) – following Artzy 1997 – proposed that they should be seen as a structural phenomenon that originated in but eventually subverted the international trade system(s) of the LBA. In her view, the LH IIIC:1b and derivative wares found in the Philistine heartland emanated from Cyprus and/or Cilicia, where they were produced and widely distributed in the eastern Mediterranean by a confederation of private maritime merchants. Bauer (2014: 31, 34), as noted earlier, also argued that the 'sea peoples' were freelance merchants – likely with multiple origins (Cyprus, Anatolia, the Aegean, Levant) – whose emergence resulted from the collapse of international trading systems. The range of material culture associated with the 'sea peoples' represents the 'international mixing' of many traditions that had circulated during the Late Bronze Age in the eastern Mediterranean as well as the emergence of a new social identity. Middleton (2018a: 100) felt that the emergence of many novel features in the early Iron Age southern Levant should be seen as a reflection of a 'post-collapse world' in which people were nonetheless still mobile and interconnected.

In a recent study considering multiple technological aspects of Philistine culture, Maeir et al. (2019: 107) argue that the appearance of some non-local technologies in the southern Levant at this time cannot be taken as a direct or even passive indicator that these foreign technologies were adopted or used in the same manner as they were in their places of origin. Instead, they may have been appropriated and transformed 'to make them relevant to the different social, economic, and identity contexts in this region at the time'. Even if some aspects (e.g. pottery, pebble hearths) were influenced by Aegean, Cypriot or even Anatolian technological traditions, others (e.g. architecture, masonry, textile production) were only partially (if at all) influenced, while still others show no influence at all (e.g. writing, chipped stone). The choices that people make – technological or otherwise – in acquiring, producing and reproducing their material culture are difficult if not impossible to associate with specific geographic, ethnic or even biological origins.

The archaeological evidence from sites all along or near the eastern Mediterranean seaboard – from Tell Tayinat in the north to Ashkelon in the south – reveals a great deal of regional chronological variability and a multivariate material culture (pottery, metal tools and weapons, chipped stone, architectural components, agricultural and plant-animal components, ivory/bone working, evidence for writing/texts). Although many archaeologists working in the southern Levant tend to overlook this variability and instead focus on regularities or similarities between often incongruent regional groups, the Levantine material evidence overall does not point to a single, uniform migratory event but instead to multiple and variant types of mobility that yield distinctive archaeological outcomes. Jumping on the genetic or isotopic bandwagon will not (soon) be able to resolve these issues: what is required instead is a deeper understanding and synthesis of the potential and limitations of each data set – material or analytical – and the capacity to assess or interpret them as distinctive albeit interconnected spheres of human activity (Furholt 2019: 125).

6 Conclusions

> What is important is that, whatever the nature of its political transformations, 'civilization' did not 'collapse'; people in the Levant continued living their Bronze Age lives until new technologies, new relations of production and new forms of political legitimacy converged in the new, Iron Age, millennium.
>
> (Greenberg 2019: 346)

Indisputably, there is good evidence for sociocultural change during the Late Bronze–early Iron Age transition in the southern Levant, around the time of the proposed Philistine migration: the material changes include ceramic traditions, food preparation and consumption practices, dress and bodily ornament, and symbolic or ceremonial practices. Even so, a substantial change in population – not to mention a mass migration – is far from evident, and there are other ways one might understand these material developments; for example, a combination of factors both external (new and different networks of exchange and the social actors involved in them) and internal (socio-economic needs during a time of crisis; politico-economic realities and shifting local preferences) (after Mac Sweeney 2017: 392–3). The most obvious innovations were not wholly external and do not invariably point to deep change; those that were external stem from diverse cultural traditions and from differing regions: Cyprus, Anatolia and the Aegean, even southeastern Europe and beyond.

To the extent that the 'sea peoples' made any impact on politico-economic development or sociohistorical change in the eastern Mediterranean at the end of the LBA, such impact should not be viewed monolithically. The breakdown in international relations and interconnections at this time must have resulted in the fragmentation of polities all along the Levantine coast, and led to new modes of interaction, both within and between polities, as well as the movement of people bearing elements of Aegean, Anatolian or Cypriot material culture. As Emanuel (2015: 22) observed: 'though newcomers are visible in the material record at some sites (but hardly all), the engagement with material influences and the negotiation of status and identity that took place across this massive area in this period were incredibly diverse in nature'.

Like the work of Sherratt, Bauer and others, this study calls into question the notion of a large-scale movement of people from the Aegean, or any other part of the Mediterranean, into the southern Levant at the end of the LBA. Unlike them, however, I would not argue that the changes evident in the material record result solely from broader, economic developments associated with private, seafaring merchants based on Cyprus or in Cilicia (the 'mercantile model'), and in particular I disagree with the notion that Cyprus became the 'powerhouse' of some coastal-based eastern Mediterranean economic and cultural system (Sherratt 1998: 294). Whereas Cyprus initially may have weathered some of the more disastrous effects of the collapse that impacted other polities in the Aegean and eastern Mediterranean during the twelfth century BC, ultimately it too felt the impact of the changing, smaller-scale, politico-economic realities of the early Iron Age (Knapp and Meyer 2020). Considering notions of migration and the aftermath of collapse in terms of entanglement, transculturation or hybridisation practices makes it possible to examine alternative dynamics involved in the seemingly widespread movements of people at the end of the LBA and the subsequent emergence of early Iron Age polities that were materially and socially distinctive from their Bronze Age antecedents.

Whereas more refined (accurate) palaeoclimatic data and more fully integrated (interdisciplinary) aDNA research hold out promise for the future, at the present time neither offer any resolution to the issues surrounding questions of migration to the southern Levant at the end of the LBA. With respect to the former, the dominant tendency is still to tack palaeoclimatic data onto existing arguments for migration. Such assertions about the link between climate change and specific human actions, events and movements – migrations or otherwise – require a much broader range of evidence employing more accurate and reliable data. With respect to the latter, as I have attempted to show through multiple examples, no matter how limited the data set or how weak the genetic signal, the current tendency is to link the results to a 'migration event' during the Late Bronze–early Iron Age transition in the southern Levant. The more significant point we should embrace from aDNA studies conducted thus far is the existence of a local Levantine gene pool spanning well over a millennium in the Bronze Age, and into the Iron Age, of the southern Levant.

As Crellin and Harris (2020: 46) argue, aDNA analyses and results, while clearly informative and important, comprise only one aspect of the relational, multivariant nature of archaeological evidence. When that evidence fails to produce compatible results in which each element of the data is in agreement, we should 'embrace a more complex and messy version where different lines of evidence tell us different things'. Even if aDNA analyses were to confirm, unanimously, that some people in the LBA southern Levant had significant amounts of European (or specifically Aegean) ancestry, this is only one aspect of understanding *who these people were, who they thought they were* and *just where they might have come from.*

The nature of human mobility is complex and multidimensional, and its socio-economic and cultural ramifications outstrip the frequency and scale over which it occurs (Woolf 2016: 463). As Leppard et al. (2020: 230–31) emphasise in their meta-analysis of strontium isotope data from funerary populations across the Neolithic to Late Roman Mediterranean (discussed previously), we should exercise caution and err on the conservative side in attempting to interpret mobility based on bioarchaeological data sets that index migration, especially when the results seem to fit poorly with prevailing models. Their concluding statement says it best (emphasis added): 'We speculate that the connected Mediterranean was a reality, but one largely limited to those with unusual social and economic wherewithal. *For the average Mediterranean villager, long-distance or frequent mobility, and certainly migration, was exceptional*'.

Issues of migration, ethnicity and identity are among the defining themes of the contemporary world, and archaeologists share a compelling if complex and inconsistent interest in all of them. Disentangling the bases and meanings of ethnicity and identity is often a fraught endeavour, and the causes, courses and outcomes of migration are as complex today as they were in the past. Written sources and iconographic evidence can certainly shed some light on ancient migrations, but often in enigmatic, programmatic or ambiguous ways. Furthermore, the spatial distribution of material traits, often adopted as a means of situating and identifying ethnic groups, is methodologically problematic, highly controversial and, in the end, inconclusive. We cannot simply assume that past migrations were limited to the movement of ethnic groups or that they only indicate demographic expansion; such movements are better regarded as specialised forms of mobility driven by specific social, environmental or historical circumstances (Hakenbeck 2008: 19).

With respect to migrants or the communities to which they moved, it is crucial for archaeologists to consider how multiple cultural meetings and mixings – the exchange of ideas, ideologies, technologies or sociocultural practices – impacted on both groups. If Bunimovitz and Lederman (2014) are correct, we may be seeing both hybridisation practices and the formation of separate communities, typically seen as separate processes. As it stands, the 'migrationist narrative' ('Philistine model') largely reflects a one-dimensional way of thinking about human mobility and social groups in the eastern Mediterranean during the LBA-early Iron Age transition, most evident in its perception of nomothetic groups (i.e. archaeological 'cultures' like the Philistines), which – contrary to the migrationist view – were not always internally homogeneous and externally sharply bounded.

As Furholt (2019: 124) pointed out in a recent study on the 'migration discourse' in third millennium BC Europe, the notion of neatly separated groups of migrants and locals, interacting or not, is a false premise. Although I question the suggestion that the 'sea peoples' were 'pirates' (Knapp 2020), it seems clear that the social groups that comprised them – *Peleset* included – were more fluid and mutable than a simplified migration model implies. As Molloy (2016: 368) observed: 'any Sea Peoples may have been less a confederation and more a constellation of shifting groups venturing into the East Mediterranean along established routes on scales that may have varied from year to year'. Thus, the interaction and mixing of locals (Canaanites) and non-locals (Philistines) was not necessarily exceptional, or even remarkable: what has been defined as migration in the case of the eastern Mediterranean at the end of the LBA is a controversial term for multiple, likely multi-generational, regional or local cases of movement, entanglement, development and demise.

References

Adams, M. J., & M. E. Cohen, 2013. The 'sea peoples' in primary sources, in *The Philistines and Other "Sea Peoples" in Text and Archaeology*, eds. A. Killebrew & G. Lehmann. (Archaeology and Biblical Studies 15.) Atlanta, GA: Society of Biblical Literature, 645–64.

Adams, W. Y., D. P. V. Gerven & R. S. Levy, 1978. The retreat from migrationism. *Annual Review of Anthropology* 7, 483–532.

Agranat-Tamir, L., S. Waldman, M. A. S. Martin . . . I. Finkelstein, L. Carmel & D. Reich (35 authors), 2020. The genomic history of the Bronze Age southern Levant. *Cell* 181, 1146–57.

Allentoft, M. E., M. Sikora, K.-G. Sjogren . . . R. Nielsen, K. Kristiansen & E. Willerslev (66 authors), 2015. Population genomics of Bronze Age Eurasia. *Nature* 522(7555),167–72. https://doi.org/10.1038/nature14507.

Ammerman, A. J., & L. L. Cavalli-Sforza, 1984. *The Neolithic Transition and the Genetics of Population in Europe*. Princeton: Princeton University Press.

Anthony, D. W., 1990. Migration in archaeology: the baby and the bathwater. *American Anthropologist* 92, 895–914.

Anthony, D. W., 1997. Prehistoric migration as social process, in *Migrations and Invasions in Archaeological Explanation*, eds. J. Chapman & H. Hamerow. (British Archaeological Reports, International Series 664.) Oxford: Tempus Reparatum, 21–32.

Artzy, M., 1997. Nomads of the sea, in *Res Maritimae: Cyprus and the Eastern Mediterranean from Prehistory through Late Antiquity*, eds. S. Swiny, R. Hohlfelder & H. W. Swiny. (Cyprus American Archaeological Research Institute, Monograph 1.) Atlanta, GA: Scholars Press, 1–16.

Artzy, M., 2006. *The Jatt Metal Hoard in Northern Canaanite/Phoenician and Cypriote Context*. (Cuadernos de Arqueología Mediterránea 14.) Barcelona: Edicions Bellaterra.

Asscher, Y., & E. Boaretto, 2018. Absolute time ranges in the plateau of the Late Bronze to Iron Age transition and the appearance of Bichrome pottery in Canaan, southern Levant. *Radiocarbon* 61: 1–25.

Aubet, M. E., 2001. *The Phoenicians and the West: Politics, Colonies and Trade*. 2nd ed. Cambridge: Cambridge University Press.

Barako, T., 2000. The Philistine settlement as mercantile phenomenon? *American Journal of Archaeology* 104, 510–30.

Barako, T. J., 2003. The changing perception of the sea peoples phenomenon: migration, invasion or cultural diffusion, in *Ploes. Sea Routes ... : Interconnections in the Mediterranean, 16th–6th C. BC*, eds. N. C. Stampolidis & V. Karageorghis. Athens: University of Crete, Leventis Foundation, 163–72.

Bauer, A., 1998. Cities of the sea: maritime trade and the origin of Philistine settlement in the Early Iron Age southern Levant. *Oxford Journal of Archaeology* 17, 149–68.

Bauer, A., 2014. The 'sea peoples' as an emergent phenomenon, in *Αθυρματα: Critical Essays on the Archaeology of the Eastern Mediterranean in Honour of E. Susan Sherratt*, eds. Y. Galanakis, T. Wilkinson & J. Bennet. Oxford: Archaeopress, 31–9.

Bellwood, P., 2013. *First Migrants: Ancient Migration in Global Perspective.* Chichester, UK:Wiley-Blackwell.

Ben-Dor Evian, S., 2015. "They were *thr* on land, others at sea ... ". The etymology of the Egyptian term for 'sea-peoples'. *Semitica* 57, 57–75.

Ben-Dor Evian, S., 2016. The battles between Ramesses III and the 'Sea-Peoples'. When, where and who?: an iconic analysis of the Egyptian reliefs. *Zeitschrift zur Ägyptischen Sprache* 143, 151–68.

Ben-Dor Evian, S., 2017. Ramesses III and the 'Sea-Peoples': towards a new Philistine paradigm. *Oxford Journal of Archaeology* 36, 267–85.

Ben-Dor Evian, S., 2018. Egyptian historiography on the mobility of (sea) people at the end of the Late Bronze Age, in *An Archaeology of Forced Migration. Crisis-Induced Mobility and the Collapse of the 13th c. BCE Eastern Mediterranean*, ed. J. Driessen. Louvain: Presses universitaires de Louvain, 219–28.

Ben-Shlomo, D., 2010. *Philistine Iconography: A Wealth of Style and Symbolism.* (Orbis Biblicus et Orientalis 241.) Fribourg: Academic Press.

Ben-Shlomo, D., I. Shai & A.M. Maeir, 2004. Late Philistine decorated ware ('Ashdod Ware'): typology, chronology, and production centers. *Bulletin of the American Schools of Oriental Research* 335, 1–35.

Ben-Shlomo, D., I. Shai, A. Zukerman & A. M. Maeir, 2008. Cooking identities: Aegean-style cooking jugs and cultural interaction in Iron Age Philistia and neighboring regions. *American Journal of Archaeology* 112, 225–46.

Bentley, R.A., 2006. Strontium isotopes from the earth to the archaeological skeleton: a review. *Journal of Archaeological Method and Theory* 13, 135–87.

Bhabha, H. K., 1994. *The Location of Culture.* London: Routledge.

Blakey, M., 2020. On the biodeterministic imagination. *Archaeological Dialogues* 27, 1–16.

Boaretto, E., Y. Asscher, L. A. Hitchcock, G. A. Lehmann, A. M. Maeir & S. Wiener, 2019. The chronology of the Late Bronze (LB) to Iron Age (IA) transition in the southern Levant: a response to Finkelstein's critique. *Radiocarbon* 61, 1–11. https://doi.org/DOI:10.1017/RDC.2018.57.

Booth, T. J., 2019. A stranger in a strange land: a perspective on archaeological responses to the palaeogenetic revolution from an archaeologist working amongst palaeogeneticists. *World Archaeology* 51, 586–601.

Bourdieu, P., 1977. *Outline of a Theory of Practice.* (Cambridge Studies in Social Anthropology 16.) Cambridge: Cambridge University Press.

Brettell, C. B., & J. F. Hollifield (eds.), 2015. *Migration Theory: Talking across Disciplines.* 3rd ed. London: Routledge.

Bronk Ramsey, C., M. W. Dee, J. M. Rowland ... E. Wild, E. S. Marcus & A. J. Shortland (10 authors), 2010. Radiocarbon-based chronology for Dynastic Egypt. *Science* 328, 1554–7.

Broodbank, C., 2014. So... what? Does the paradigm currently want to budge so much? *Journal of Mediterranean Archaeology* 27, 267–71.

Bunimovitz, S., 1990. Problems in the "ethnic" identification of the Philistine culture. *Tel Aviv* 17, 210–22.

Bunimovitz, S., 1998. Sea Peoples in Cyprus and Israel: a comparative study of immigration processes, in *Mediterranean Peoples in Transition: Thirteenth to Tenth Centuries BCE*, eds. S. Gitin, A. Mazar & E. Stern. Jerusalem: Israel Exploration Society, 103–13.

Bunimovitz, S., & Z. Lederman, 2014. Migration, hybridization, and resistance: identity dynamics in the early iron age southern Levant, in *The Cambridge Prehistory of the Bronze and Iron Age Mediterranean*, eds. A. B. Knapp & P. van Dommelen New York: Cambridge University Press, 252–65.

Bunimovitz, S., & A. Yasur-Landau, 1996. Philistine and Israelite pottery: a comparative approach to the question of pots and people. *Tel Aviv* 23, 88–101.

Bunimovitz, S., & A. Yasur-Landau, 2002. Women and Aegean immigration to Cyprus in the 12th century BCE, in *Engendering Aphrodite: Women and Society in Ancient Cyprus*, eds. D. Bolger & N. Serwint. (CAARI Monograph 3.) Boston: American Schools of Oriental Research, 211–22.

Burmeister, S., 2000. Archaeology and migration: approaches to an archaeological proof of migration. *Current Anthropology* 41, 539–67.

Burmeister, S., 2017. The archaeology of migration: what can and should it accomplish?, in *Migration und Integration von Der Urgeschichte bis zum Mittelalter – Migration and Integration from Prehistory to the Middle Ages.* (Tagungen des Landesmuseum für Vorgeschichte Halle 17.) Halle, Germany: Landesmuseum für Vorgeschichte, 57–68.

Cabana, G., & J. Clark, 2011. Introduction. Migration in anthropology: where we stand, in *Rethinking Anthropological Perspectives on Migration*, eds. G. Cabana & J. Clark. Gainesville: University Press of Florida, 3–15.

Cameron, C. M., 1995. Migration and the movement of southwestern peoples. *Journal of Anthropological Archaeology* 14, 104–24.

Carter, T., D. A. Contreras, J. Holcomb ... N. Taffin, D. Athanasoulis & C. Lahaye (9 authors), 2019. Earliest occupation of the central Aegean (Naxos), Greece: implications for hominin and Homo sapiens' behavior and dispersals. *Science Advances* 5(10: eaax0997), 1–9. https://advances.sciencemag.org/content/5/10/eaax0997.

Chapman, J., & H. Hamerow (eds.), 1997. *Migrations and Invasions in Archaeological Explanation*. (British Archaeological Reports, International Series 664.) Oxford: Tempus Reparatum.

Cherry, J. F., & T. P. Leppard, 2018. Patterning and its causation in the pre-Neolithic colonization of the Mediterranean islands (Late Pleistocene to Early Holocene). *Journal of Island and Coastal Archaeology* 13, 191–205.

Childe, V. G., 1928. *The Most Ancient East: The Oriental Prelude to European Prehistory*. London: Kegan Paul, Trench, Trubner.

Childe, V. G., 1950. *Prehistoric Migrations in Archaeology*. Oslo: Aschehoug and Co.

Clark, G. A., 1994. Migration as an explanatory concept in Paleolithic archaeology. *Journal of Archaeological Method and Theory* 1, 305–43.

Clarke, D. L., 1968. *Analytical Archaeology*. London: Methuen.

Cline, E. H., 1994. *Sailing the Wine-Dark Sea: International Trade and the Late Bronze Age Aegean*. (British Archaeological Reports, International Series 591.) Oxford: Archaeopress.

Comaroff, J. L., & J. Comaroff, 1992. *Ethnography and the Historical Imagination*. Boulder, CO: Westview Press.

Crellin, R. J., & O. J. T. Harris, 2020. Beyond binaries: interrogating ancient DNA. *Archaeological Dialogues* 27, 37–56.

Cross, F. M., & L. E. Stager, 2006. Cypro-Minoan inscriptions found in Ashkelon. *Israel Exploration Journal* 56, 129–59.

Cusick, J. G., 1998. Historiography of acculturation: an evaluation of concepts and their application in archaeology, in *Studies in Culture Contact: Interaction, Culture Change and Archaeology*, ed. J. G. Cusick. (Center For Archaeological Investigations, Occasional Paper 25.) Carbondale: Southern Illinois University Press, 126–45.

Davis, B., 2018. What language(s) did the Philistines speak? *Near Eastern Archaeology* 81, 22–23.

Davis, B., A. M. Maeir & L. A. Hitchcock, 2015. Disentangling entangled objects: Iron Age inscriptions from Philistia as a reflection of cultural processes. *Israel Exploration Journal* 65, 140–66.

Diaz-Andreu, M., 1997. Nationalism, ethnicity and archaeology: the archaeological study of Iberians through the looking glass. *Journal of Mediterranean Studies* 7, 154–68.

Diaz-Andreu, M., S. Lucy, S. Babic & D. N. Edwards, 2005. *The Archaeology of Identity: Approaches to Gender, Age, Status, Ethnicity and Religion.* London: Routledge.

Dothan, M., 1986. Shardina at Akko?, in *Studies in Sardinian Archaeology II: Sardinia in the Mediterranean*, ed. M. Balmuth. Ann Arbor: University of Michigan Press, 105–15.

Dothan, T., 1982. *The Philistines and Their Material Culture.* New Haven and London: Yale University Press.

Dothan, T., 1998. Initial Philistine settlement: from migration to coexistence, in *Mediterranean Peoples in Transition: Thirteenth to Tenth Centuries BCE*, eds. S. Gitin, A. Mazar & E. Stern. Jerusalem: Israel Exploration Society, 148–61.

Dothan, T., 2000. Reflections on the initial phase of Philistine settlement, in *The Sea Peoples and Their World: A Reassessment*, ed. E. Oren. (University Museum Monograph 108.) Philadelphia: University Museum, University of Pennsylvania, 145–58.

Dothan, T., & M. Dothan, 1992. *People of the Sea: The Search for the Philistines.* New York: Macmillan.

Dothan, T., & A. Zukerman, 2004. A preliminary study of the Mycenaean IIIC:1 pottery assemblages from Tel Miqne-Ekron and Ashdod. *Bulletin of the American Schools of Oriental Research* 333, 1–54.

Drews, R., 1993. *The End of the Bronze Age: Changes in Warfare and the Catastrophe of ca. 1200 BC.* Princeton: Princeton University Press.

Drews, R., 2000. Medinet Habu: oxcarts, ships and migration theories. *Journal of Near Eastern Studies* 59, 161–90.

Driessen, J. (ed.), 2018. *An Archaeology of Forced Migration: Crisis-Induced Mobility and the Collapse of the 13th c. BCE Eastern Mediterranean.* Louvain: Presses universitaires de Louvain.

Eisenmann, S., E. Bánffy, P. van Dommelen … J. Krause, D. Reich & P. W. Stockhammer (11 authors), 2018. Reconciling material cultures in archaeology with genetic data: the nomenclature of clusters emerging from archaeogenomic analysis. *Scientific Reports* 8(13003),1–12. https://www.nature.com/articles/s41598-018-31123-z

Emanuel, J. P., 2015. King Taita and his "Palistin": Philistine state or Neo-Hittite kingdom? *Antiguo Oriente* 13, 11–40.

Emanuel, J. P., 2016. 'Sea Peoples' in Egyptian garrisons in light of Beth-Shean, (re-) reconsidered. *Mediterranean Archaeology* 28/29, 1–21.

Emberling, G., 1997. Ethnicity in complex societies: archaeological perspectives. *Journal of Archaeological Research* 5, 295–344.

Faust, A., 2018. Pigs in space (and time): pork consumption and identity negotiations in the Late Bronze and Iron Ages of ancient Israel. *Near Eastern Archaeology* 81, 276–99.

Faust, A., 2019. 'The inhabitants of Philistia': on the identity of the Iron I settlers in the periphery of the Philistine heartland. *Palestine Exploration Quarterly* 151, 105–33.

Faust, A., & J. Lev-Tov, 2011. The constitution of Philistine identity: ethnic dynamics in twelfth to tenth century Philistia. *Oxford Journal of Archaeology* 30, 13–31.

Feldman, M., D. M. Master, R. A. Bianco ... A. J. Aja, C. Jeong & J. Krause (9 authors), 2019. Ancient DNA sheds light on the genetic origins of early Iron Age Philistines. *Science Advances* 5(eaax0061), 1–10. https://advances.sciencemag.org/content/5/7/eaax0061

Finkelstein, I., 1996. Ethnicity and origin of the Iron I settlers in the highlands of Canaan: can the real Israel stand up? *Biblical Archaeologist* 59, 198–213.

Finkelstein, I., 2000. The Philistine settlements: when, where and how many?, in *The Sea Peoples and Their World: A Reassessment*, ed. E. D. Oren. (University Museum Monograph 108. University Museum Symposium Series 11.) Philadelphia: The University Museum, University of Pennsylvania, 159–80.

Finkelstein, I., 2007. Is the Philistine paradigm still viable?, in *The Synchronisation of Civilisations in the Eastern Mediterranean in the Second Millennium BC III*, eds. M. Bietak & E. Czerny. (Denkschrfiten der Gesamtakademie 37. Contributions to the Chronology of the Eastern Mediterranean 9.) Wein: Verlag der Österreichischen Akademie der Wissenschaften, 517–23.

Finkelstein, I., 2016. To date or not to date: radiocarbon and the arrival the Philistines. *Ägypten und Levante* 26, 275–84.

Finkelstein, I., D. Langgut, M. Meiri & L. Sapir-Hen, 2017. Egyptian imperial economy in Canaan: reaction to the climate crisis at the end of the Late Bronze Age. *Ägypten und Levante* 27, 249–60.

Finné, M., K. Holmgren, H. S. Sundqvist, E. Weiberg & M. Lindblom, 2011. Climate in the eastern Mediterranean, and adjacent regions, during the past 6000 years: a review. *Journal of Archaeological Science* 38, 3153–73.

Finné, M., K. Holmgren, C.-C. Shen, H.-M. Hu, M. Boyd & S. Stocker, 2017. Late Bronze Age climate change and the destruction of the

Mycenaean Palace of Nestor at Pylos. *PLoS ONE* 12(12),e0189447. https://journals.plos.org/plosone/article?id=10.1371/journal.pone.0189447

Finné, M., J. Woodbridge, I. Labuhn & C. N. Roberts, 2019. Holocene hydro-climatic variability in the Mediterranean: a synthetic multi-proxy reconstruction. *The Holocene* 29, 847–63.

Fischer, P. M. & T. M. Bürge (eds.), 2017. *'Sea Peoples' Up-to-Date: New Research on Transformation in the Eastern Mediterranean in the 13th–11th Centuries BCE.* Wein: Verlag der Österreichischen Academie der Wissenschaften.

Furholt, M., 2018. Massive migrations? The impact of recent aDNA studies on our view of third millennium Europe. *European Journal of Archaeology* 21, 159–91.

Furholt, M., 2019. Re-integrating archaeology: a contribution to aDNA studies and the migration discourse on the 3rd millennium BC in Europe. *Proceedings of the Prehistoric Society* 85, 115–29.

Furholt, M., 2020. Biodeterminism and pseudo-objectivity as obstacles for the emerging field of archaeogenetics. *Archaeological Dialogues* 27, 23–5.

Gadot, Y., 2019. The Iron I settlement wave in the Samaria highlands and its connection with the urban centers. *Near Eastern Archaeology* 82, 32–41.

Galanidou, N., 2018. Parting the waters: Middle Palaeolithic archaeology in the central Ionian Sea. *Journal of Greek Archaeology* 2, 1–22.

Gilboa, A., 2005. Sea Peoples and Phoenicians along the southern Phoenician coast – a reconciliation: an interpretation of Sikila (SKL) material culture. *Bulletin of the American Schools of Oriental Research* 337, 47–78.

Gilboa, A., & I. Sharon, 2017. Fluctuations in Levantine maritime foci across the Late Bronze/Iron Age transition: charting the role of the Sharon-Carmel (Tjeker) coast in the rise of Iron Age Phoenician polities, in *'Sea Peoples' Up-To-Date: New Research on Transformation in the Eastern Mediterranean in the 13th-11th Centuries BCE*, eds. P. M. Fischer & T. Bürge. Wein: Verlag der Österreichischen Akademie der Wissenschaften, 285–98.

Gitin, S., 2004. The Philistines: neighbors of the Canaanites, Phoenicians and Israelites, in *One Hundred Years of American Archaeology in the Middle East*, eds. D. Clark & V. Matthews. Boston: American Schools of Oriental Research, 57–84.

Gitin, S., T. Dothan & J. Naveh, 1997. A royal dedicatory inscription from Ekron. *Israel Exploration Journal* 47, 1–16.

Goody, J., 2001. Bitter icons. *New Left Review* 7, 5–15.

Greenberg, R., 2019. *The Archaeology of the Bronze Age Levant: From Urban Origins to the Demise of City-States, 3700–1000 BCE.* Cambridge: Cambridge University Press.

Greenblatt, S. (ed.), 2010. *Cultural Mobility: A Manifesto*. Cambridge: Cambridge University Press.

Gregoricka, L. A., & Sheridan, S. G., 2017. Continuity or conquest? A multi-isotope approach to investigating identity in the Early Iron Age of the southern Levant. *American Journal of Physical Anthropology* 162, 73–89.

Gur-Arieh, S., E. Boaretto, A. M. Maeir & R. Shahack-Gross, 2012. Formation processes in Philistine hearths from Tell es-Safi/Gath (Israel): an experimental approach. *Journal of Field Archaeology* 37, 121–31.

Haak, W., I. Lazaridis, N. Patterson, ..., A. Cooper, K. W. Alt & D. Reich (39 authors), 2015. Massive migration from the steppe was a source for Indo-European languages in Europe. *Nature* 522, 207–11.

Haber, M., C. Doumet-Serhal, C. Scheib, ..., P. Zalloula, T. Kivisild & C. Tyler-Smith (16 authors), 2017. Continuity and admixture in the last five millennia of Levantine history from ancient Canaanite and present-day Lebanese genome sequences. *American Journal of Human Genetics* 101, 274–82.

Hakenbeck, S., 2008. Migration in archaeology: are we nearly there yet? *Archaeological Review from Cambridge* 23(2), 9–26.

Hakenbeck, S., 2019. Genetics, archaeology and the far right: an unholy Trinity. *World Archaeology* 51, 517–27.

Hamilakis, Y. (ed.), 2018. *The New Nomadic Age: Archaeologies of Forced and Undocumented Migration*. Sheffield: Equinox.

Hastorf, C. A., 2017. *The Social Archaeology of Food: Thinking about Eating from Prehistory to the Present*. Cambridge: Cambridge University Press.

Hawkins, J. D., 2000. *Corpus of Hieroglyphic Luwian Inscriptions 1. Inscriptions of the Iron Age*. (Studies in Indo-European Languages and Culture n.s. 3 [3 vols.].) Berlin: de Gruyter.

Hawkins, J. D., 2020. The Hieroglyphic Luwian inscriptions of the Amuq, in *Alalakh and Its Neighbours*, eds. K. A. Yener & T. Ingman. (Ancient Near Eastern Studies Supplement 55.) Louvain: Peeters, 41–53.

Hegmon, M., 1998. Technology, style, and social practices: archaeological approaches, in *The Archaeology of Social Boundaries*, ed. M. T. Stark. Washington, DC: Smithsonian Institution Press, 264–79.

Hesse, B., & P. Wapnish, 1997. Can pig remains be used for ethnic diagnosis in the Ancient Near East?, in *The Archaeology of Israel: Constructing the Past, Interpreting the Present*, eds. N. A. Silberman & D. B. Small. (Journal for the Study of the Old Testament, Supplement 237.) Sheffield: Sheffield Academic Press, 238–70.

Hitchcock, L. A., & A. M. Maeir, 2013. Beyond creolization and hybridity: entangled and transcultural identities in Philistia. *Archaeological Review from Cambridge* 28(1), 51–72.

Hitchcock, L. A., & A. M. Maeir, 2014. Yo-ho, yo-ho, a seren's life for me! *World Archaeology* 46, 624–40.

Hodder, I.A., 1982. *Symbols in Action: Ethnoarchaeological Studies of Material Culture*. Cambridge: Cambridge University Press.

Hofmann, D., 2019. Review of D. Reich, *Who We Are and How We Got Here: Ancient DNA and the New Science of the Human Past* (Oxford, 2018). *European Journal of Archaeology* 22, 434–7.

Hoffmeier, J. K., 2018. A possible location in northwest Sinai for the sea and land battles between the Sea Peoples and Ramesses III. *Bulletin of the American Schools of Oriental Research* 380, 1–25.

Iacovou, M., 2013. Aegean-style material culture in Late Cypriot III: minimal evidence, maximal interpretation, in *The Philistines and Other "Sea Peoples" in Text and Archaeology*, eds. A. Killebrew & G. Lehmann. (Archaeology and Biblical Studies 15.) Atlanta, GA: Society of Biblical Literature, 585–618.

Ingman, T., S. Eisenmann, E. Skourtanioti ... P. Roberts, K. A. Yener & P. W. Stockhammer (17 authors), 2020. Human mobility at Tell Atchana (Alalakh) during the 2nd millennium BC: integration of isotopic and genomic evidence. www.biorxiv.org/content/10.1101/2020.10.23.351882v1.

Janeway, B., 2017. *Sea Peoples of the Northern Levant? Aegean-Style Pottery from Early Iron Age Tell Tayinat*. (Studies in the Archaeology and History of the Levant 7.) Winona Lake, IN: Eisenbrauns.

Joffe, A. H., 2002. The rise of secondary states in the Iron Age Levant. *Journal of the Economic and Social History of the Orient* 45: 425–67.

Jones, S., 1997. *The Archaeology of Ethnicity: Reconstructing Identities in the Past and the Present*. London: Routledge.

Jung, R., 2017. The sea peoples after three millennia: possibilities and limitations of historical reconstruction, in *'Sea Peoples' Up-To-Date: New Research on Transformation in the Eastern Mediterranean in the 13th–11th Centuries BCE*, eds. P. M. Fischer & T. M. Bürge. Wein: Verlag der Österreichischen Akademie der Wissenschaften, 23–42.

Jung, R., 2018. Push and pull factors of the sea peoples between Italy and the Levant, in *An Archaeology of Forced Migration. Crisis-Induced Mobility and the Collapse of the 13th c. BCE Eastern Mediterranean*, ed. J. Driessen. Louvain: Presses universitaires de Louvain, 273–306.

Kahn, D., 2011. The campaign of Ramesses III against Philistia. *Journal of Ancient Egyptian Interconnections* 3–4, 1–11.

Kaniewski, D., E. Paulissen, E. Van Campo, H. Weiss, T. Otto, J. Bretschneider & K.V. Lerberghe, 2010. Late second–early first millennium BC abrupt climate changes in coastal Syria and their possible significance for the history of the Eastern Mediterranean. *Quaternary Research* 74, 207–215.

Kaniewski, D., E. Van Campo, K. V. Lerberghe … C. Morhange, T. Otto & J. Bretschneider (9 authors), 2011. The Sea Peoples, from cuneiform tablets to carbon dating. *PLoS ONE* 6(6), 1–7. e20232

Kaniewski, D., E. Van Campo, J. Guiot, S. La Bruel, T. Otto and C. Baeteman, 2013. Environmental roots of the Late Bronze Age crisis. *PLoS ONE* 8(8),1–10. e71004.

Kaniewski, D., N. Marriner, J. Bretschneider … T. Otto, F. Luce & E. Van Campo (9 authors), 2019. 300-year drought frames Late Bronze Age to Early Iron Age transition in the Near East: new palaeoecological data from Cyprus and Syria. *Regional Environmental Change* 19: 2287–97. https://link.springer.com/article/10.1007/s10113-018-01460-w

Kaniewski, D., & E. Van Campo, 2017. The climatic context of the 3.2 kyr Cal BP event, in *'Sea Peoples' Up-To-Date: New Research on Transformation in the Eastern Mediterranean in the 13th–11th Centuries BCE*, eds. P. M. Fischer & T. M. Bürge. Wein: Verlag der Österreichischen AKademie der Wissenschaften, 85–94.

Karageorghis, V., 2013. Cyprus at the end of the Bronze [Age] again. *Pasiphae* 7, 125–32.

Karageorghis, V., 2019. *New Archaeological Evidence for 12th Century BC Nicosia*. (Ledraika.) Nicosia: Leventis Foundation.

Killebrew, A., 2005. *Biblical Peoples and Ethnicity: An Archaeological Study of Egyptians, Canaanites, Philistines, and Early Israel 1300–1100 BCE*. Atlanta, GA: Society of Biblical Literature.

Killebrew, A.E., 2018a. From "global" to "glocal": cultural connectivity and interactions between Cyprus and the southern Levant during the transitional Late Bronze and Early Iron Ages, in *Change, Continuity, and Connectivity. North-Eastern Mediterranean at the Turn of the Bronze Age and in the Early Iron Age*, eds. J. L. Niesiołowski-Spanò & P. M. Węcowski. (Philippika 118.) Wiesbaden: Harrassowitz, 81–94.

Killebrew, A., 2018b. The Levant in crisis: the materiality of migrants, refugees and colonizers at the end of the Bronze Age, in *An Archaeology of Forced Migration. Crisis-Induced Mobility and the Collapse of the 13th c. BCE Eastern Mediterranean*, ed. J. Driessen. Louvain: Presses universitaires de Louvain, 187–202.

Knapp, A. B., 1973. Mycenaean Pottery at Ugarit: Some Historical and Chronological Reflections. Unpublished MA thesis, Near Eastern Studies, University of California, Berkeley.

Knapp, A. B., 2001. Archaeology and ethnicity: a dangerous liaison. *Archaeologia Cypria* 4, 29–46.

Knapp, A. B., 2008. *Prehistoric and Protohistoric Cyprus: Identity, Insularity and Connectivity.* Oxford: Oxford University Press.

Knapp, A. B., 2014. Mediterranean archaeology and ethnicity, in *A Companion to Ethnicity in the Ancient Mediterranean*, ed. J. Mcinerney. Oxford: Wiley Blackwell, 34–49.

Knapp, A. B., 2020. Piracy in the Late Bronze Age eastern Mediterranean? A cautionary tale. In A. Gilboa and A. Yasur-Landau, eds., *Nomads of the Mediterranean: Trade and Contact in the Bronze and Iron Ages. Studies in Honor of Michal Artzy*, 142–60. Leiden: Brill.

Knapp, A. B., & J. F. Cherry, 1994. *Provenience Studies and Bronze Age Cyprus: Production, Exchange, and Politico-Economic Change.* (Monographs in World Archaeology 21.) Madison, WI: Prehistory Press.

Knapp, A. B., & S. W. Manning, 2016. Crisis in context: the end of the Late Bronze Age in the eastern Mediterranean. *American Journal of Archaeology* 120, 99–149.

Knapp, A. B. & N. Meyer, 2020. Cyprus: Bronze Age demise, Iron Age regeneration, in *Collapse and Transformation: The Late Bronze Age to Early Iron Age in the Aegean*, ed. G. D. Middleton. Oxford: Oxbow Books, 237–46.

Krauss, R., 2015. Egyptian chronology: Ramesses II through Shoshenq III, with analysis of the lunar dates of Tuthmoses III. *Ägypten und Levante* 25, 335–82.

Kristiansen, K., 2014. Towards a new paradigm? The third science revolution and its possible consequences in archaeology. *Current Swedish Archaeology* 22, 11–34.

Kristiansen, K., 2016. Interpreting Bronze Age trade and migration, in *Human Mobility and Technological Transfer in the Prehistoric Mediterranean*, eds. E. Kiriatzi & C. Knappett. Cambridge: Cambridge University Press, 154–80.

Kristiansen, K., M. E. Allentoft, K. M. Frei … K.-G. Sjögren, M. Sikora & E. Willerslev (12 authors), 2017. Re-theorising mobility and the formation of culture and language among the Corded Ware Culture in Europe. *Antiquity* 91 (356), 334–47.

Kuhrt, A., 1996. *The Ancient Near East: c. 3000–330 BC.* London: Routledge.

Langgut, D., I. Finkelstein & T. Litt, 2013. Climate and the Late Bronze collapse: new evidence from the southern Levant. *Tel Aviv* 40, 149–75.

Lehmann, G., 2017. The Late Bronze-Iron Age transition and the problem of the sea peoples phenomenon in Cilicia, in *'Sea Peoples' Up-To-Date: New Research on Transformation in the Eastern Mediterranean in the 13th–11th Centuries BCE*, eds. P. M. Fischer & T. M. Bürge. Wein: Verlag der Österreichischen Adademie der Wissenschaften, 229–56.

Leppard, T.P., 2014. Mobility and migration in the Early Neolithic of the Mediterranean: questions of motivation and mechanism. *World Archaeology* 46, 484–501.

Leppard, T. R., C. Esposito & M. Esposito, 2020. The bioarchaeology of migration in the ancient Mediterranean: meta-analysis of radiogenic (87Sr/86Sr) isotope ratios. *Journal of Mediterranean Archaeology* 33 (2): 211–41.

Mac Sweeney, N., 2017. Separating fact from fiction in the Ionian migration. *Hesperia* 86, 379–421.

MacArthur, R. H. & E. O. Wilson, 1967. *The Theory of Island Biogeography*. Princeton: Princeton University Press.

Maeir, A. M. & L. A. Hitchcock, 2011. Absence makes the hearth grow fonder: searching for the origins of the Philistine hearth, in *Amnon Ben-Tor Volume*, eds. J. Aviram, S. Gitin, A. Mazar, N. Na'Aman, E. Stern & S. Zuckerman. (Eretz Israel 30.) Jerusalem: Israel Exploration Society, Hebrew University of Jerusalem, 46*–64*.

Maeir, A. M. & Hitchcock, L. A., 2017. The appearance, formation and transformation of Philistine culture: new perspectives and new finds, in *'Sea Peoples' Up-to-Date: New Research on Transformation in the Eastern Mediterranean in the 13th–11th Centuries BCE*, eds. P. M. Fischer & T. Bürge. Wein: Verlag der Österreichischen Akademie der Wissenschaften, 149–62.

Maeir, A. M., B. David & L. A. Hitchcock, 2016. Philistine names and terms once again: a recent perspective. *Journal of Eastern Mediterranean Archaeology and Heritage Studies* 4, 321–40.

Maeir, A. M., D. Ben-Shlomo, D. Cassuto ... E. Weiss, E. L. Welch & V. Workman (16 authors), 2019. Technological insights on Philistine culture. *Journal of Eastern Mediterranean Archaeology and Heritage Studies* 7, 76–118.

Manning, S. W., C. Kearns & B. Lorentzen, 2017. Dating the end of the Late Bronze Age with radiocarbon: some observations, concerns, and revisiting the dating of Late Cypriot IIC to IIIA, in *'Sea Peoples' Up-To-Date: New Research on Transformation in the Eastern Mediterranean in the 13th–11th Centuries BCE*, eds. P. M. Fischer & T. Bürge. Wein: Verlag der Österreichischen Akademie der Wissenschaften, 95–110.

Marcus, J. H., C. Posth, H. Ringbauer, ..., F. Cucca, J. Krause & J. Novembre (38 authors), 2020. Genetic history from the Middle Neolithic to present on the Mediterranean island of Sardinia. *Nature Communications* 11: 939. https://www.nature.com/articles/s41467-020-14523-6.

Martîn García, J. M., & M. Artzy, 2018. Cultural transformations shaping the end of the Late Bronze Age in the Levant, in *Proceedings of the 10th International Congress on the Archaeology of the Ancient Near East*, eds.

B. Horejs, C. Schwall, V. Müller, M. Luciani, M. Ritter, M. Guidetti, R. B. Salisbury, F. Höflmayer & T. Bürge. Wiesbaden: Harrassowitz, 97–106.

Master, D. M., & A. J. Aja, 2017. The Philistine cemetery of Ashkelon. *Bulletin of the American Schools of Oriental Research* 377, 135–59.

Matić, U., & F. Francović, 2020. Sea Peoples and the discourse of 'Balkanism' in Late Bronze Age archaeology, in *Spheres of Interaction: Contacts and Relationships between the Balkans and Adjacent Regions in the Late Bronze / Iron Age (13th–5th Centuries BCE)*, eds. M. Gavranović, D. Heilmann, A. Kapuran & M. Verčík. Rahden/Westfallen: Verlag Marie Leidorf, 155–76.

Matisoo-Smith, E., A. L. Gosling, R.A. Bianco . . . G. Abou Diwan, J. Nassar & P. Zalloua (17 authors), 2018. Ancient mitogenomes of Phoenicians from Sardinia and Lebanon: a story of settlement, integration, and female mobility. *PLoS ONE* 13 (1):e0190169. https://journals.plos.org/plosone/article?id=10.1371/journal.pone.0190169.

Mazar, A., 1985. The emergence of the Philistine material culture. *Israel Exploration Journal* 35, 95–107.

Meiberg, L., 2013. Philistine lion-headed cups: Aegean or Anatolian?, in *The Philistines and Other 'Sea Peoples' in Text and Archaeology*, eds. A. Killebrew & G. Lehmann. (Archaeology and Biblical Studies 15.) Atlanta, GA: Society of Biblical Literature, 131–44.

Meiri, M., D. Huchon, G. Bar-Oz . . . G. Larsen, S. Weiner & I. Finkelsetin (10 authors), 2013. Ancient DNA and population turnover in southern Levantine pigs: signature of the sea peoples migration? *Scientific Reports* 3(3035),1–8. https://doi.org/10.1038/srep03035.

Meiri, M., P. W. Stockhammer, N. Marom . . . D. Huchon, J. Maran & I. Finkelstein (11 authors), 2017. Eastern Mediterranean mobility in the Bronze and Early Iron Ages: inferences from ancient DNA of pigs and cattle. *Scientific Reports* 7(701),1–10. https://doi.org/10.1038/s41598-017-00701-y

Meiri, M., P. W. Stockhammer, P. Morgenstern & J. Maran, 2019. Mobility and trade in Mediterranean antiquity: evidence for an 'Italian connection' in Mycenaean Greece revealed by ancient DNA of livestock. *Journal of Archaeological Science, Reports* 23, 98–103.

Middleton, G. D., 2015. Telling stories: the Mycenaean origin of the Philistines. *Oxford Journal of Archaeology* 34, 45–65.

Middleton, G.D., 2018a. 'I would walk 500 miles and I would walk 500 more': the Sea Peoples and Aegean migration at the end of the Late Bronze Age, in *Change, Continuity, and Connectivity: North-Eastern Mediterranean at the Turn of the Bronze Age and in the Early Iron Age*, eds. J. L. Niesiołowski-

Spanò & P. M. Węcowski. (Philippika 118.) Wiesbaden: Harrassowitz, 95–115.

Middleton, G. D., 2018b. Should I stay or should I go? Mycenaeans, migration, and mobility in the Late Bronze Age and Early Iron Age eastern Mediterranean. *Journal of Greek Archaeology* 3, 115–43.

Middleton, G. D., 2019. Collapse of Bronze Age civilizations, in *Climate Changes in the Holocene: Impacts and Human Adaptation*, ed. E. Chiotis. Boca Raton, FL: CRC Press, 271–92.

Middleton, G. (ed.), 2020. *Collapse and Transformation: The Late Bronze Age to Early Iron Age in the Aegean*. Oxford: Oxbow.

Millek, J. M., 2018. Destruction and the fall of Egyptian hegemony over the southern Levant. *Journal of Ancient Egyptian Interconnections* 19, 1–21.

Millek, J. M., 2019. *Exchange, Destruction, and a Transitioning Society: Interregional Exchange in the Southern Levant from the Late Bronze Age to the Iron I*. (Ressourcen Kulturen 9.) Tübingen: Tübingen University Press.

Mithen, S., 2018. Neanderthals, Denisovians and modern humans. Review of D. Reich, *Who We Are and How We Got Here: Ancient DNA and the New Science of the Human Past* (Oxford, 2018), *London Review of Books* 40(17), 3–6.

Molloy, B. P. C., 2016. Nought may endure but mutability: eclectic encounters and material change in the 13th to 11th centuries BC Aegean, in *Of Odysseys and Oddities: Scales and Modes of Interaction between Prehistoric Aegean Societies and Their Neighbours*, ed. B. P. C. Molloy. (Sheffield Studies in Aegean Archaeology 10.) Oxford: Oxbow, 343–83.

Monroe, C., 2018. Marginalizing civilization: the Phoenician redefinition of power ca. 1300–800 BC, in *Trade and Civilisation: Economic Networks and Cultural Ties, from Prehistory to the Early Modern Era*, eds. K. Kristiansen, T. Lindkvist & J. Myrdal. Cambridge: Cambridge University Press, 195–241.

Mountjoy, P., 1998. The east Aegean-west Anatolian interface in the Late Bronze Age: Mycenaeans and the kingdom of Ahhiyawa. *Anatolian Studies* 48, 33–67.

Mountjoy, P., 2010. A note on the mixed origins of some Philistine pottery. *Bulletin of the American Schools of Oriental Research* 359, 1–2.

Mountjoy, P., 2015. The east Aegean-west Anatolian interface in the 12th century BC. Some aspects arising from the Mycenaean pottery, in *NOSTOI: Indigenous Culture, Migration and Integration in the Aegean Islands and Western Anatolia during the Late Bronze and Early Iron Ages*, eds. N. C. Stampolidis, Ç. Maner & K. Kopanias. (Koç University Press Archaeology 58.) Istanbul: Koç University Press, 37–80.

Mountjoy, P., 2018. *Decorated Pottery in Cyprus and Philistia in the 12th Century BC: Cypriot IIIC and Philistine IIIC.* 2 vols. Wein: Verlag der Österreichischen Akademie der Wissenschaften.

Muhly, J. D., 1980. Bronze figurines and Near Eastern metalwork. *Israel Exploration Journal* 30, 148–61.

Muhly, J. D., 1984. The role of the Sea Peoples in Cyprus during the LC III period, in *Cyprus at the Close of the Late Bronze Age*, eds. V. Karageorghis & J. D. Muhly. Nicosia: Leventis Foundation, 39–55.

Nafplioti, A., 2016. Late Minoan IB destructions and cultural upheaval on Crete: a bioarchaeological perspective, in *Population Dynamics in Prehistory and Early History: New Approaches Using Stable Isotopes and Genetics*, eds. E. Kaiser, J. Burger & W. Schier. (Topoi 5.) Berlin: De Gruyter, 241–63.

Osborne, J., 2013. Sovereignty and territoriality in the city–state: a case study from the Amuq Valley, Turkey. *Journal of Anthropological Archaeology* 32, 774–90.

Osborne, J. F., T. P. Harrison, S.Batiuk, L. Welton, J. P. Dessell, E. Denel and Ö. Demirci, 2019. Urban built environments in early 1st milllennium BCE Syro-Anatolia: results of the Tayinat Archaeological Project, 2004–2016. *Bulletin of the American Schools of Oriental Research* 38, 261–312.

Palmisano, A., J. Woodbridge, C. N. Roberts … S. A. G. Leroy, T. Litt & A. Miebach (13 authors), 2019. Holocene landscape dynamics and long-term population trends in the Levant. *The Holocene* 29, 708–27.

Panitz-Cohen, N., 2014. The southern Levant (Cisjordan) during the Late Bronze Age, in *The Oxford Handbook of the Archaeology of the Levant c. 8000–323 BCE*, eds. A. E. Killebrew & M. L. Steiner. Oxford: Oxford University Press, 541–60.

Pfoh, E., 2018. Socio-political changes and continuities in the Levant (1300–900 BCE, in *Change, Continuity, and Connectivity. North-Eastern Mediterranean at the Turn of the Bronze Age and in the Early Iron Age.*, eds. J. L. Niesiołowski-Spanò & P. M. Węcowski. (Philippika 118.) Wiesbaden: Harrassowitz, 57–67.

Raban, A. & Y. Tur-Caspa, 2008. Underwater survey, 1985–1987, in *Ashkelon I. Introduction and Overview (1985–2006)*, eds. L. E. Stager, J. D. Schloen & D. M. Master. Winona Lake, IN: Eisenbrauns, 67–96.

Rahmstorf, L., 2011. Handmade pots and crumbling loomweights: 'barbarian' elements in the Eastern Mediterranean in the last quarter of the 2nd millennium BC, in *On Cooking Pots, Drinking Cups, Loomweights and Ethnicity in Bronze Age Cyprus and Neighbouring Regions*, eds. V. Karageorghis & O. Kouka. Nicosia: Leventis Foundation, 315–30.

Raneri, S., F. Venturi, V. Palleschi, S. Legnaioli, M. Lezzerini, S. Pagnotta, M. Ramacciotti & G. Gallello, 2019. Social and technological changes in the ceramic production of the northern Levant during the LBA/IA transition: new evidence about the Sea People issue through archaeometry. *Journal of Anthropological Archaeology* 56 (101087). https://www.sciencedirect.com/science/article/pii/S0278416518302290.

Reich, D., 2018. *Who We Are and How We Got Here: Ancient DNA and the New Science of the Human Past.* Oxford: Oxford University Press.

Renfrew, A. C., 1987. *Archaeology and Language: The Puzzle of Indo-European Origins.* London: Jonathan Cape.

Renfrew, C., & K. Boyle (eds.), 2000. *Archaeogenetics: DNA and the Population Prehistory of Europe.* Cambridge: McDonald Institute for Archaeological Research.

Robb, J., 2016. Introduction: the archaeology of bodies and the Eastern Mediterranean, in *An Archaeology of Prehistoric Bodies and Embodied Identities in the Eastern Mediterranean*, eds. M. Mina, S. Triantaphyllou & Y. Papadatos. Oxford: Oxbow, vii–xii.

Roberts, R. G., 2009. Identity, choice, and the Year 8 reliefs of Ramesses III at Medinet Habu, in *Forces of Transformation: The End of the Bronze Age in the Mediterranean*, eds. C. Bachhuber & R. G. Roberts. (BANEA Publication Series 1.) Oxford: Oxbow, 60–8.

Rouse, I., 1986. *Migrations in Prehistory.* New Haven and London: Yale University Press.

Routledge, B., 2017. Is there an Iron Age Levant? *Revista del Instituto de Historia Antigua Oriental* 18, 49–76.

Runnels, C., 2014. Early Palaeolithic on the Greek Islands? *Journal of Mediterranean Archaeology* 27, 211–30.

Russell, A., 2009. Deconstructing Ashdoda: migration, hybridisation, and the Philistine identity. *BABESCH* 84, 1–15.

Sader, H., 2019. *The History and Archaeology of Phoenicia.* Atlanta, GA: SBL Press.

Sandars, N. K., 1978. *The Sea Peoples: Warriors of the Ancient Mediterranean 1250–1150 BC.* London: Thames and Hudson.

Sapir-Hen, L., 2019. Food, pork consumption, and identity in ancient Israel. *Near Eastern Archaeology* 82, 52–9.

Sapir-Hen, L., G. Bar-Oz, Y. Gadot & I. Finkelstein, 2013. Pig husbandry in Iron Age Israel and Judah: new insights regarding the origin of the 'taboo'. *Zeitschrift des Deutschen-Palästina Vereins* 129, 1–20.

Sapir-Hen, L., M. Meiri & I. Finkelstein, 2015. Iron Age pigs: new evidence on their origin and role in forming identity boundaries. *Radiocarbon* 57, 307–15.

Seguin, J., J. Bintliff, P. M. Grootes . . . E. M. Wild, E. Zagana & I. Unkel (13 authors), 2019. 2500 years of anthropogenic and climatic landscape transformation in the Stymphalia Polje, Greece. *Quaternary Science Reviews* 213, 133–54.

Sharon, I., 2001. Philistine Bichrome painted pottery: scholarly ideology and ceramic typology, in *Studies in the Archaeology of Israel and Neighboring Lands in Memory of Douglas L. Esse*, ed. S. R. Wolff. (Studies in Ancient Oriental Civilizations 59.) Boston: American Schools of Oriental Research, 555–609.

Sharon, I., & A. Gilboa, 2013. The skl town: Dor in the Early Iron Age, in *The Philistines and Other 'Sea Peoples' in Text and Archaeology*, eds. A. Killebrew & G. Lehmann. (Archaeology and Biblical Studies 15.) Atlanta, GA: Society of Biblical Literature, 393–468.

Sherratt, E. S., 1992. Immigration and archaeology: some indirect reflections, in *Acta Cypria 2*, ed. P. Astrom. (Studies in Mediterranean Archaeology and Literature, Pocketbook 117.) Jonsered, Sweden: P. Åström's Förlag, 316–47.

Sherratt, S., 1998. 'Sea peoples' and the economic structure of the late second millennium in the eastern Mediterranean, in *Mediterranean Peoples in Transition: Thirteenth to Tenth Centuries BCE*, eds. S. Gitin, A. Mazar & E. Stern. Jerusalem: Israel Exploration Society, 292–313.

Sherratt, S., 2003. The Mediterranean economy: 'globalization' at the end of the second millennium BCE, in *Symbiosis, Symbolism, and the Power of the Past: Canaan, Ancient Israel, and Their Neighbors, from the Late Bronze Age through Roman Palaestina*, eds. W. G. Dever and S. Gitin. Winona Lake, IN: Eisenbrauns, 37–62.

Sherratt, S., 2005. 'Ethnicities' 'ethnonyms' and archaeological labels. Whose ideologies and whose identities?, in *Archaeological Perspectives on the Transmission and Transformation of Culture in the Eastern Mediterranean*, ed. J. Clarke. Oxford: Oxbow, 25–38.

Sherratt, S., 2013. The ceramic phenomenon of the 'sea peoples': an overview, in *The Philistines and Other "Sea Peoples" in Text and Archaeology*, eds. A. Killebrew & G. Lehmann. (Archaeology and Biblical Studies 15.) Atlanta, GA: Society of Biblical Literature, 619–44.

Sherratt, S., 2016. From "institutional" to "private": traders, routes and commerce from the Late Bronze Age to the Iron Age, in *Dynamics of Production in the Ancient Near East*, ed. J. C. M. Garcia. Oxford: Oxbow, 289–302.

Silberman, N.A., 1998. The Sea Peoples, the Victorians and us: modern social ideology and changing archaeological interpretations of the Late Bronze Age collapse, in *Mediterranean Peoples in Transition: Thirteenth to Tenth*

Centuries BCE, eds. S. Gitin, A. Mazar & E. Stern. Jerusalem: Israel Exploration Society, 268–75.

Singer, I., 2012. The Philistines in the north and the kingdom of Taita, in *The Ancient Near East in the 12th–10th Centuries BCE: Culture and History*, eds. G. Galil, A. Gilboa, A.M. Maeir & D. Kahn. (Alter Orient und Altes Testament 392.) Münster: Ugarit-Verlag, 451–72.

Stager, L., 1995. The impact of the Sea Peoples in Canaan (1185–1050 BCE), in *The Archaeology of Society in the Holy Land*, ed. T.E. Levy. Leicester: Leicester University Press, 332–48.

Stern, E., 2000. The Sea Peoples in northern Israel, in *The Sea Peoples and Their World: A Reassessment*, ed. E. D. Oren. (University Museum Monograph 108. University Museum Symposium Series 11.) Philadelphia: The University Museum, University of Pennsylvania, 197–212.

Stern, E., 2013. *The Material Culture of the Northern Sea Peoples in Israel.* (Studies in the Archaeology and History of the Levant 5.) Winona Lake, IN: Eisenbrauns.

Stockhammer, P.W., 2018. Rethinking Philistia as a contact zone, in *Tell It in Gath: Studies in the History and Archaeology of Israel. Essays in Honor of Aren M. Maeir on the Occasion of His Sixtieth Birthday*, eds. Y. Shai, J. R. Chadwick, L. Hitchcock, A. Dagan, C. Mckinny & J. Uziel. (Ägypten und Altes Testament 90.) Münster: Zaphon, 375–84.

Stone, B.J., 1995. The Philistines and acculturation: culture change and ethnic continuity in the Iron Age. *Bulletin of the American Schools of Oriental Research* 298, 7–32.

Strasser, T. G., E. Panagopoulou, C.N. Runnels, P. M. Murray, N. Thomspon, P. Karkanas, F. T. McCoy & K. W. Wegmann, 2010. Stone Age seafaring in the Mediterranean: evidence from the Plakias region for Lower Palaeolithic and Mesolithic habitation of Crete. *Hesperia* 79, 145–90.

Strasser, T. G., C. N. Runnels, K. W. Wegmann, E. Panagopoulou, F. T. McCoy, C. Degregoria, P. Karkanas & N. Thomspon, 2011. Dating Palaeolithic sites in southwestern Crete, Greece. *Journal of Quaternary Science* 26, 553–60.

Sweeney, D., & A. Yasur-Landau, 1999. Following the path of the Sea Persons: the women in the Medinet Habu reliefs. *Tel Aviv* 26, 116–45.

Sykes, N., M. Spriggs & A. Evin, 2019. Beyond curse or blessing: the opportunities and challenges of aDNA analysis. *World Archaeology* 51, 503–16.

Tanasi, D., & N. Vella, 2014. Islands and mobility: exploring Bronze Age connectivity in the south-central Mediterranean, in *The Cambridge Prehistory of the Bronze and Iron Age Mediterranean*, eds. A. B. Knapp & P. van Dommelen. New York: Cambridge University Press, 57–73.

Trigger, B. G., 1968. *Beyond History: The Methods of Prehistory*. New York: Holt, Rinehart and Winston.

Tyerman, C., 2006. *God's War: A New History of the Crusades*. Cambridge, MA: Harvard University Press.

Ullinger, J., S. Sheridan, D. Hawkey, C. Turner-Walker & R. Cooley, 2005. Bioarchaeological analysis of cultural transition in the southern Levant using dental nonmetric traits. *American Journal of Physiological Anthropology* 128, 466–76.

Uziel, J., 2007. The development process of Philistine material culture: assimilation, acculturation and everything in between. *Levant* 39, 165–73.

van den Bergh, G., Y. Kaifu, I. Kurniawan, R. T. Kono, A. Brumm, E. Setiyabudi, F. Aziz and M. J. Morwood, 2016. *Homo floresiensis*-like fossils from the early Middle Pleistocene of Flores. *Nature* 534, 245–48.

van Dommelen, P., 2012. Colonialism and migration in the ancient Mediterranean. *Annual Review of Anthropology* 41, 393–409.

van Dommelen, P., 2014. Moving on: archaeological perspectives on mobility and migration. *World Archaeology* 46, 477–83.

van Dommelen, P., 2018. Trading places? Sites of mobility and migration in the Iron Age West Mediterranean, in *The Emporion in the Ancient Western Mediterranean: Trade and Colonial Encounters from the Archaic to the Hellenistic Period*, eds. E. Gailledrat, M. Dietler & R. Plana-Mallart. Montpellier: Presses universitaires de la Méditerranée, 219–29.

van Dommelen, P., & A. B. Knapp (eds.), 2010. *Material Connections in the Ancient Mediterranean: Mobility, Materiality and Identity*. London: Routledge.

Van Oyen, A., 2017. Material culture and mobility: a brief history of archaeological thought, in *Mobility and Pottery Production: Archaeological and Anthropological Perspectives*, eds. C. Heitz & R. Stapfer. Leiden: Sidestone Press, 53–65.

Vander Linden, M., 2007. What linked the Bell Beakers in third millennium BC Europe? *Antiquity* 81(312), 343–52.

Vander Linden, M., 2016. Population history in third-millennium-BC Europe: assessing the contribution of genetics. *World Archaeology* 48, 714–28.

Vanschoonwinkel, J., 1999. Between the Aegean and the Levant: the Philistines, in *Ancient Greeks West and East*, ed. G. R. Tsetskhladze. Leiden: Brill, 85–108.

Verduci, J., 2018. *Metal Jewellery of the Southern Levant and Its Western Neighbours: Cross-Cultural Influences in the Early Iron Age Eastern Mediterranean*. (Ancient Near Eastern Studies, Supplement 53.) Leuven: Peeters.

Verduci, J. (2019). A feather in your cap: symbols of "Philistine" warrior status?, in *Fashioned Selves: Dress and Identity in Antiquity*, ed. M. Cifarelli. Oxford: Oxbow, 131–46.

Vernet Pons, M., 2012. The etymology of Goliath in the light of Carian PN WLJAT / WLIAT: a new proposal. *Kadmos* 51, 143–64.

Voskos, I., & A. B. Knapp, 2008. Cyprus at the end of the Late Bronze Age: crisis and colonization, or continuity and hybridization? *American Journal of Archaeology* 112, 659–84.

Wachsmann, S., 1998. *Seagoing Ships and Seamanship in the Bronze Age Levant*. College Station: Texas A&M University Press.

Wachsmann, S., 2008. Underwater survey, 1996–1997, in *Ashkelon I. Introduction and Overview (1985–2006)*, eds. L. E. Stager, J. D. Schloen & D. M. Master. Winona Lake, IN: Eisenbrauns, 97–100.

Wachsmann, S., 2013. *The Gurob Ship-Cart Model and Its Mediterranean Context*. College Station: Texas A&M University Press.

Weeden, M., 2013. After the Hittites: the kingdoms of Karkamish and Palistin in northern Syria. *Bulletin of the Institute of Classical Studies* 56(2),1–20.

Weiberg, E., & M. Finné, 2018. Resilience and persistence of ancient societies in the face of climate change: a case study from Late Bronze Age Peloponnese. *World Archaeology* 50: 584–602.

Welton, L., T. Harrison, S.D. Batiuk ... D. Lipovitch, D. Lumb & J. Roames (9 authors), 2019. Shifting networks and community identity at Tell Tayinat in the Iron I (ca. 12th to mid 10th century B.C.E.). *America Journal of Archaeology* 123, 291–333.

Woolf, G., 2016. Movers and stayers, in *Migration and Mobility in the Early Roman Empire*, eds. L. de Ligt & L. E. Tacoma. (Studies in Global Social History 23/7.) Leiden: Brill, 440–63.

Yahalom-Mack, N., 2019. Crucibles, tuyères, and bellows in a longue durée perspective: aspects of technological style. *Journal of Eastern Mediterranean Archaeology and Heritage Studies* 7, 63–75.

Yasur-Landau, A., 2005. Old wine in new vessels: intercultural contact, innovation and Aegean, Canaanite and Philistine foodways. *Tel Aviv* 32, 168–91.

Yasur-Landau, A., 2010. *The Philistines and Aegean Migration at the End of the Late Bronze Age*. Cambridge: Cambridge University Press.

Yasur-Landau, A., 2012a. The 'feathered helmets' of the Sea Peoples: joining the iconographic and archaeological evidence. *Talanta* 44, 27–40.

Yasur-Landau, A., 2012b. The role of the Canaanite population in the Aegean migration to the southern Levant in the late second millennium BCE, in *Materiality and Social Practice: Transformative Capacities of Intercultural Encounters*, eds. J. Maran & P. Stockhammer. Oxford: Oxbow, 191–7.

Yasur-Landau, A., 2013. Chariots, spears and wagons: Anatolian and Aegean elements in the Medinet Habu land battle relief, in *The Ancient Near East in the 12th to 10th Centuries BCE: Culture and History*, eds. G. Galil, A. Gilboa, A. M. Maeir & D. Kahn. (Alter Orient und Altes Testament 392.) Münster: Ugarit-Verlag, 549–68.

Yasur-Landau, A., 2018. Towards an archaeology of forced movement of the deep past, in *An Archaeology of Forced Migration. Crisis-Induced Mobility and the Collapse of the 13th c. BCE Eastern Mediterranean*, ed. J. Driessen. Louvain: Presses universitaires de Louvain, 177–85.

Zuckerman, S., 2007. Anatomy of a destruction: crisis architecture, termination rituals and the fall of Canaanite Hazor. *Journal of Mediterranean Archaeology* 20, 3–32.

Zuckerman, S., 2008. Fit for a (not-quite-so-great) king: a faience lion-headed cup from Hazor. *Levant* 40, 115–25.

Zukerman, A., 2011. Titles of 7th century B.C.E. Philistine rulers and their historical-cultural background. *Bibliotheca Orientalis* 68, 465–71.

About the Author

A. Bernard Knapp is Emeritus Professor of Mediterranean Archaeology in the Department of Humanities (Archaeology), University of Glasgow, and Honorary Research Fellow, Cyprus American Archaeological Research Institute, Nicosia. He co-edits the *Journal of Mediterranean Archaeology* with John F. Cherry and Peter van Dommelen and is general editor of the series *Monographs in Mediterranean Archaeology*. He is the author or editor of several books including, most recently, *Seafaring and Seafarers in the Bronze Age Eastern Mediterranean* (Leiden, Sidestone Press, September 2018).

Acknowledgments

I am grateful to Guy Middleton, Michal Artzy and Thomas Leppard for reading and commenting on an earlier draft of this manuscript. I also thank Philipp Stockhammer for his comments on an earlier draft of the section on palaeogenetics. My thanks to Nathan Meyer for producing the maps and several other figures, and to Timothy Harrison, Aren Maeir, Sturt Manning, Linda Meiberg, Anthony Russell, Susan Sherratt and Josephine Verduci for providing figures. Shlomo Bunimovitz had also agreed to read an earlier draft of this work, but his (fatal) illness prevented him from doing so. Although he might not have been particularly pleased about it, I would like to dedicate this volume to his memory, and to all his exemplary research – including the Philistines – on the Bronze Age archaeology of the southern Levant.

Cambridge Elements ≡

The Archaeology of Europe

Manuel Fernández-Götz

University of Edinburgh

Manuel Fernández-Götz is Reader in European Archaeology and Head of the Archaeology Department at the University of Edinburgh. In 2016 he was awarded the prestigious Philip Leverhulme Prize. His main research interests are Iron Age and Roman archaeology, social identities and conflict archaeology. He has directed fieldwork projects in Spain, Germany, the United Kingdom and Croatia.

Bettina Arnold

University of Wisconsin–Milwaukee

Bettina Arnold is Full Professor of Anthropology at the University of Wisconsin–Milwaukee and Adjunct Curator of European Archaeology at the Milwaukee Public Museum. Her research interests include the archaeology of alcohol, the archaeology of gender, mortuary archaeology, Iron Age Europe and the history of archaeology.

About the Series

Elements in the Archaeology of Europe is a collaborative publishing venture between Cambridge University Press and the European Association of Archaeologists. Composed of concise, authoritative, and peer-reviewed studies by leading scholars, each volume in this series will provide timely, accurate, and accessible information about the latest research into the archaeology of Europe from the Paleolithic era onwards, as well as on heritage preservation.

$$\begin{matrix} E \\ A \\ A \end{matrix}$$ European Association *of* Archaeologists

Cambridge Elements ≡

The Archaeology of Europe

Elements in the Series

Printed in the United States
by Baker & Taylor Publisher Services